DOOMED BOURGEOIS IN LOVE

Whit Stillman

Doomed Bourgeois in Love

Essays on the Films of
Whit Stillman

edited by Mark C. Henrie

ISI Books • Wilmington, Delaware • 2001

Five of the essays collected here, chapters 1, 3, 4, 6, and 9, originally appeared in a symposium in the *Intercollegiate Review,* vol. 35, no. 2 (Spring 2000), and are reprinted with the permission of the Intercollegiate Studies Institute. To these have been added four original essays written for this volume: chapters 2, 5, 7, and 8.

Four reviews which appeared at the time of the film and book releases are also reprinted in an appendix. "Metropolitan" is reprinted by with the permission of Luc Sante. "Places in the Heart" is reprinted with the permission of Donald Lyon. "Call it Cosmpolitan" is reprinted with the permission of Armond White. "Whit Stillman: Novelist" is reprinted with the permission of *The American Spectator.*

Cataloging-in-Publication Data:

Doomed bourgeois in love : essays on the films of Whit Stillman /
    edited by Mark C. Henrie. --1st ed, --Wilmington, Del. : ISI Books, 2001.

     p. cm.

    ISBN 1-882926-70-6 (pbk.)
      1. Stillman, Whit, 1952--Criticism and interpretation.
      2. Motion pictures--United States--History and criticism.
      I. Henrie, Mark C. II. Essays on the Films of Whit Stillman

PN1993.5.U6 D66 2001   2001-087969
791.43/0233/092--dc21   CIP

Published in the United States by:

ISI Books
Post Office Box 4431
Wilmington, DE 19807-0431
www.isibooks.org

Manufactured in the United States of America

"You're obviously talking about a lot more than detachable collars...."

"Yeah, I am."

—from *Metropolitan*

Contents

Notes on Contributors   ix

Introduction: At Whit's End   xi
     Mark C. Henrie

One   Whit Stillman's Comic Art   1
     Mary P. Nichols

Two   Whit Stillman's Restorative Irony   19
     Lauren Weiner

Three   Whit Stillman: Poet of the Broken Branches   39
     James Bowman

Four   From Mansfield to Manhattan:
     The Abandoned Generation of *Metropolitan*   49
     R. V. Young

Five   In Defense of Virtue:
     Whit Stillman's *Metropolitan*   63
     Joseph Alulis

Six   Europe and America in *Barcelona*   87
           E. Christian Kopff

Seven   Text and Subtext in *Barcelona*   99
           Mark C. Henrle

Eight   The Apotheosis of Disco   119
           David M. Whalen

Nine   Nature, Grace, and *The Last Days of Disco* 133
           Peter Augustine Lawler

Appendix: Selected Previously Published Reviews
           Metropolitan   149
           Luc Sante

           Places in the Heart   154
           Donald Lyon

           Call it Cosmopolitan   161
           Armond White

           Whit Stillman, Novelist   167
           George Sim Johnston

Index   171

Notes on Contributors

Joseph Alulis teaches political science at North Park University in Chicago. He is the co-editor of *Tocqueville's Defense of Human Liberty* (1993) and of *Shakespeare's Political Pageant* (1996). He has published scholarly articles on Shakespeare, Tocqueville, and Lincoln.

James Bowman is American Editor of the *Times Literary Supplement*, media critic for the *New Criterion*, and film critic for the *American Spectator*.

Mark C. Henrie is Senior Editor at the Intercollegiate Studies Institute and Senior Editor of *Modern Age: A Quarterly Review*. He is author of *A Student's Guide to the Core Curriculum* (ISI Books, 2000).

E. Christian Kopff is Professor of Classics and Associate Director of the Honors Program at the University of Colorado, editor of a critical edition of the Greek text of Euripides' *Bacchae*, and author of *The Devil Knows Latin: Why America Needs the Classical Tradition* (ISI Books, 1999).

Peter Augustine Lawler is Professor of Government at Berry College in Georgia. Among his many and diverse publications are *Postmodernism Rightly Understood: The Return to Realism in American Thought* (1999) and the forthcoming *Aliens in America: The Strange Truth about Our Souls* (ISI Books, 2002). He is the editor of the quarterly journal *Perspectives on Political Science*.

Mary P. Nichols is Professor of Political Science at Fordham University. She has published widely in the history of political thought, especially Greek political thought. Her interests include politics and literature, and politics and film. She is the author of *Socrates and the Political Community* (1987), *Citizens and Statesmen: A Study of Aristotle's* Politics (1992), and *Reconstructing Woody: Art, Love, and Life in the Films of Woody Allen* (1998).

Lauren Weiner has written on literature and politics for the *New Criterion*, the *Weekly Standard*, the *Wall Street Journal*, *Society*, and many other publications. She works on Capitol Hill in Washington as editor for Senator Jon Kyl.

David M. Whalen is Associate Professor of English and Dean of the Faculty at Hillsdale College. He is the author of *The Consolation of Rhetoric: John Henry Newman and the Realism of Personalist Thought* (1994). He has also published articles and essays on Chaucer, Shakespeare, Dickens, and liberal education.

R. V. Young is Professor and Director of Graduate Programs in the Department of English at North Carolina State University. His books include *At War With the Word* (ISI Books, 1999), *A Student's Guide to Literature* (ISI Books, 1999), and *Doctrine and Devotion in Seventeenth-Century Poetry* (2000).

AT WHIT'S END

Mark C. Henrie

DOOMED. BOURGEOIS. IN LOVE.

With those words, used in advertising copy to promote the 1990 Academy Award-nominated *Metropolitan*, Whit Stillman debuted his peculiar comic genius. At once class-conscious, theory-laden, nostalgically romantic, and deflatingly ironic, Stillman has charmed thousands (though he doubtless hoped for millions) of viewers. Such enchantment is an unexpected sensation for today's ironical "bourgeois bohemians," who are otherwise given to dismissing sentimentality in art. The affectionate mood so successfully conveyed by the films thus presents a puzzle, as does the maze of hyper-reflective dialogue which tends to overshadow the plots— perhaps by design. At first amused by the earnest conversations of his characters, we begin at length to realize that Stillman is playing a deeper game than we had suspected. Themselves charmed, and therefore intrigued, by Stillman's art, the writers gathered here have each applied their considerable critical intelligences in an effort to uncover the purposes so cleverly hidden in the comedy.

Nicely turned out in dinner jackets and evening gowns, Stillman's smart set in *Metropolitan* discourse loquaciously—and in self-consciously perfect syntax—about their own demise. The film takes us into the privileged drawing rooms of Manhattan's Upper East Side during the Christmas debutante season where, to our surprise, we encounter "basically...good [people]."* It would appear that the only villain in this world of mannered innocents is a titled German aristocrat who mocks manners as something unserious. But there is another villain: time itself. The timeless moment of "the season" passes, dissolving the Sally Fowler Rat Pack. But more seriously, as the grand social theorizing which constitutes an astonishing portion of the film's dialogue suggests, the passage of historical time seems to doom those echoes of chivalric romance which stir at least a few of these quasi-aristocratic souls. Yet "doomed" is not the last word here; love is.

Barcelona (1994) then chronicles the encounter of two very American cousins with the wiles and seductions of an old Europe now promiscuously new. While both manners and morals give rise to comic inversions, the serious question the film raises concerns the nature of patriotism as a human excellence. The radical Spanish journalist's cosmopolitan sophistication neglects the fact that cultured prosperity is secured by the unsophisticated courage of those who are willing to put themselves at physical risk for the defense of others. And as American boys winning the hands of Spanish women in marriage demonstrates in the end, the love of familiar ways is no insuperable bar to an attraction for the Other.

The conclusion of Stillman's trilogy, *The Last Days of Disco* (1998), portrays a group of Harvard graduates in their first jobs

---

*Throughout this volume, unless otherwise indicated, the writers have quoted from Stillman's actual movies. The shooting scripts as written by Stillman are also available, however, and some of the writers make use of these to clarify points in the films. The scripts of Stillman's first two movies were published as *Barcelona and Metropolitan: Tales of Two Cities* (Faber and Faber, 1994).

after college who take up with two Hampshire graduates working in publishing. Where for others the disco scene involved an unrestrained embrace of the culture of sex and drugs, here the main attraction is "the exchange of ideas and points of view"—on such subjects as the interpretation of animated Disney features—and the return of the civilizing influence of music one can dance to. The heroine, whose virtues exceed all others in her social group, learns at last that love is a grace which can perfect us as it overcomes our *amour propre*. But what is more, we learn in the film that beyond all manners and convention, this grace abounds for those who have ears to hear.

What brings unity to these films as a trilogy is of course Stillman's filmmaking art, an unostentatious realism that turns our attention to what his characters are saying—to the *word*. But the other source of unity is the human type they chronicle. The urban haute bourgeoisie (or "U.H.B." or "uhbs") as they are called in *Metropolitan* were known in "better" days simply as the gentlefolk. Democratic and meritocratic America has never had much time for gentility, and radical ideologies in principle despise the well-born. For these reasons, the gentlefolk tend to appear in our popular art either as villains or as fools. But Stillman's films insist that there were (and are) true virtues to be found in this class and its ideals. The manners of *Metropolitan*, the courage of *Barcelona*, the opening to grace of *Last Days*—each captures a facet of a kind of knight-errantry which is a permanent human possibility. And by the genius of Stillman's irony, he has *shown* the humane gentleness of his subjects in such a way that we end up simply liking them, despite all our prejudices against them. Villains they are not, and their foolishness is readily forgiven.

Stillman himself is from an elite socio-economic background. He is a graduate of Harvard College who has lived in Barcelona and once worked in publishing. He has an enduring appreciation for disco music. Clearly, he writes about what he knows. But in so doing, he has hit upon an exceptionally useful device to explore the possibilities and limitations, in a democratic age, of human beings as such. In each of his films, Stillman provides a highly reflective portrayal of the lives, loves, and longings of the high-born class who in another time would have been the serenely self-confident carriers of aristocratic tradition. Under democracy, the status of this class is profoundly in doubt—as are the very ideals and virtues that the aristocrats claimed to represent. While necessarily touched by anxiety, Stillman's young men and women at least remain aware of a rumor of the noble and the gracious, of the higher things which are properly human. Thus, oddly, Stillman's rare specimens may be closer to human nature than are we. But like all of us, the gentlefolk suffer the disorientation of modernity, the loss of tradition. The perplexity that animates each of Stillman's films is how to find our way, how to live well, when the cake of custom has been broken. And what is most striking in Stillman as he confronts our common predicament is his standpoint of gentle hope.

Each film in the trilogy concerns an ending, a passing away. In *Metropolitan*, the characters lament that they are living through the last debutante season as they know it, one already "pretty much reduced" from earlier years. *Barcelona* takes place in "the last decade of the Cold War." And a sense of ending is explicit in the faux-apocalyptic title of *The Last Days of Disco*. In each of the films a wistful nostalgia colors everything. While our progressive civilization dismisses "mere" nostalgia out of hand, Stillman strives to give nostalgia its due. For such a feeling arises from a powerful intuition of the human good which is revealed in its passing away. Knowledge of that passing good should stir us to affection—and away from cynicism—for to know the human good is to know an essence that can never finally pass away. History does not have the last word. As Ted Boynton explains in *Barcelona*, Americans are deni-grated in Europe because it is known they love hamburgers, which are terrible in Europe. But hamburgers really are great in America, and "it is that ideal burger of memory we crave." Great burgers, of course, are real. Perhaps so too our longings for a remembered, better past also point to something real. Such a *comic* sensibility can lead us beyond nostalgia and pain of loss: it contains the germ of action. The great critic Allen Tate glimpsed as much when he observed, "The most that we can do with the past is to salvage what is good in the present and hold on to it; and that creates a new past."

Now, such ponderous thoughts must not obscure the fact that Stillman's films are *comedies*. They are usually thought to be com-edies of manners, but that is likely not correct. In a typical comedy of manners, conventional people confront situations which try the resources of conventional manners to the breaking point. But this is not the source of the delight in Stillman's films. How could it be in an age which has unsettled all manners, when there are no con-ventional resources to be tapped, let alone strained? Stillman's char-acters, moreover, are self-conscious about the plight of convention in the modern world in a way which unsuits them to the traditional unreflective roles in a comedy of manners. If anything, Stillman's films might be classified as comedies of *mannerlessness*. And yet, they are not grim or black comedies; far from it.

That we live in a time of disruption, of the hollowing out of old beliefs, manners, and traditions, is an intuition shared by many twentieth-century artists in every field and of every political per-suasion. Such a diagnosis of the age lay behind T. S. Eliot's great modernist poem, "The Wasteland." The same view inspired ab-stract expressionism in the visual arts as well as the American dra-matists of mid-century. Such an intuition leads many architects today to build avowedly ugly buildings, since to do otherwise (it is said) would be to "hide" the harsh realities of modern life with mere "pastiche." In an age of spiritual crisis, confident and celebratory genres such as the epic become an impossibility. As these examples indicate, a discordant and *tragic* retelling of the human condition would seem in the first instance to be the appropriate artistic response to the disruptive spirits of the late-modern or postmodern age. But that is not Stillman's response. While seeming to agree substantially with this diagnosis of our spiritual malady, Stillman's *comic* art resembles instead that of the novelist Walker Percy. In fact, the title of one of Percy's comic masterpieces, *Love in the Ruins*, captures nicely the essence of Stillman's trilogy. We may hope for redemption after all.

In his warmly affectionate embrace of all his flawed and sometimes foolish characters, in his abiding hope in the power of friendship and love, and in the chorus of quixotic commentary that peppers the dialogue, Stillman reveals himself as something like a latter-day Christian humanist. Perhaps in an age such as ours, it is not tragedy but *comedy* which is the truly illuminating artistic response. Not the ridicule-ridden ancient comedy of an Aristophanes, but the gentle and ironic comedy of a Thomas More. When the action of Stillman's trilogy is arranged chronologically, *Barcelona*, not *Last Days*, is the final act; and as in Shakespeare, the comedy concludes with a multiple marriage—an affirmation of the potentially sublime goodness of human love. At present such comedy is a rarified taste, but its discreet charm may lead one day to a common grace.

One

WHIT STILLMAN'S COMIC ART

Mary P. Nichols

WHIT STILLMAN HAS CLAIMED that he does not want to make serious dramas, only comedies. This does not mean, however, that his work has no serious intention. Critics have classified his three films, *Metropolitan*, *Barcelona*, and *The Last Days of Disco*, as comedies of manners, and are reminded of Jane Austen. And well they might be, for Stillman has admitted that Austen, along with Tolstoy and Samuel Johnson, are the authors he loves most. A comedy of manners, according to the dictionary definition, is a satirical treatment of conventional or fashionable society. Satire arises when an author places an outsider among those who take the fashions, customs, and attitudes of their class for granted, allowing the audience to see conventional society from the outsider's perspective. In Austen's *Pride and Prejudice*, for example, we watch along with Mr. Bennet the absurdities of his wife's efforts to introduce their daughters into fashionable society. Comedy lies in the discrepancy between that society's understanding of itself and what the outsider sees. In a way, a comedy of manners portrays fashionable society itself as a version of the classic comic figure, the boaster, at whom the audience laughs when the discrepancy between his pretensions and the truth comes to light.

Comedies of manners, however, need not be simply critical of the manners they satirize. While the English society of *Pride and Prejudice* offers us the hypocritical Miss Bingley, it also offers us Mr. Darcy, whose character and life reveal a sensitivity and moral worth inconceivable without society. Elizabeth Bennet may be an outsider whose keen perception penetrates Miss Bingley, but then so is Elizabeth's sister Lydia, whose scorn for conventions leads to disgrace. Nor is it possible to understand Stillman's comedy without exploring the ambiguity of his attitude toward his characters, captured by one reviewer as "mocking affection."

In *Metropolitan*, we see a group of Manhattan socialites through the eyes of outsider Tom Townsend (Edward Clements), a Westsider among the Eastsider elites, a disciple of the French socialist Charles Fourier, a reader of Thorstein Veblen, and one opposed to debutante parties on principle. One of the debutantes of the group, Audrey Rouget (Carolyn Farina), is herself a kind of outsider, due in part to her love of Jane Austen. When Tom objects that "everything Jane Austen wrote seems ridiculous from today's perspective," Audrey is quick to respond: "Has it ever occurred to you that today, looked at from Jane Austen's perspective, would look much worse?" By the end of the movie, Tom comes to appreciate Austen, Audrey, and his new friends.

In *Barcelona*, Ted and Fred Boynton (Taylor Nichols and Chris Eigeman) are American innocents abroad, one in the office of an American company in Barcelona, the other a naval officer on a diplomatic assignment there. However much they try to belong to the Spanish social scene, they are bourgeois Americans trying to negotiate European culture and corruption, as well as anti-American political sentiment. Their unsophisticated tastes and sexual mores, their capitalist values, their American patriotism, and even their old-fashioned piety at first appear ridiculous, especially in the eyes of their Spanish friends, but ultimately constitute their solid human decency. The movie suggests a bridge between the two cultures when Ted's business requires commuting between Barcelona and Chicago, and eventually both Ted and Fred marry foreign women and bring them to the States.

The preppies of *Metropolitan* have become yuppies in *The Last Days of Disco*, and they frequent an exclusive Manhattan disco club. They are all now more or less outside, constantly trying to get into the Club. Even the Club's underboss occupies a precarious status, constantly risking his job by admitting friends through the back door. Stillman presents the conventions of disco culture, and the social craze it represents, as ridiculous, and certainly as morally questionable as the fashionable society of Austen's novels. But while the fashions of any age may be limited and timebound, Stillman lets us see the human aspirations moving his characters' attraction to disco, just as Austen herself illustrates the moral benefits of social conventions. In this essay, I shall explore Stillman's comic standpoint in his three films—a standpoint that makes Stillman himself a mocking but affectionate critic, an outsider who is not simply an outsider.

*M*etropolitan shows us Manhattan debutantes and their escorts home for Christmas vacation from their Ivy League schools. Scenes occur primarily at all-night "afterparties" in the affluent living rooms of the "urban haute bourgeoisie," or the U.H.B., a term coined by the group's theoretician, Charlie (Taylor Nichols). The film is well described as one of "preppy angst." Stillman shows us Spengler's *Decline of the West* by Tom's bedside as he dresses in his tuxedo. Another of the escorts laments the changing social conditions that foretell the "last deb season as we know it." Another senses that their whole preppy class is "doomed" to failure and extinction. Or perhaps their angst must be understood in less world historical terms, for as they themselves recognize, they are "at a very vulnerable point in their lives."

Metropolitan opens with the tears of its heroine, insecure deb Audrey Rouget, who is having difficulty with the fit of her new evening dress. Her mother tries to comfort her with the thought that her younger brother is no authority on female anatomy. Mrs. Rouget can at least take in the dress where "it is a bit full." As Mrs. Rouget knows, her daughter's dress may be altered, not so that it hides defects but so that it allows strengths to appear to best advantage. Hers is an art motivated by love.

Audrey comes to like her group's newcomer Tom, although he claims that Austen's *Mansfield Park* is "a notoriously bad book." Tom is initially the critic not only of Austen, but of the whole debutante scene. Falling in with the snobbish and sophisticated SFRP (the Sally Fowler Rat Pack, as they call themselves after one of their group), Tom is a less "haute" bourgeois. He rents rather than owns his tuxedo, and he intends to go to no more dances—until Nick Smith (Chris Eigeman) changes his mind.

Nick also advises Tom about the dress code, defending the use of detachable collars in men's formal evening dress—"a small thing, but symbolically important," he informs Tom, observing that "our parents' generation was never interested in keeping up standards." Although such collars "look much better," like many things they "have been abandoned for supposed convenience." Although Stillman encourages us to smile at Nick's concern with detachable collars, he lets Nick's remarks about standards echo later in the movie when Nick himself has to admit that he has "failed to live up to [the standards of the U.H.B.]."

Nick's failure lay in telling a story about Polly Perkins—a young woman whom Nick claims was mistreated by the movie's cad Rick von Sloneker (Will Kempe). But Polly Perkins is "a fabrication," and von Sloneker accuses Nick of lying. Even Nick's friend Charlie tells him "this looks really bad." Nick insists that Polly Perkins is a composite rather than a fabrication, for while there is no one Polly, "there're many of them." But von Sloneker's view prevails with the Rat Pack. While Frank Sinatra's rat pack, from which Sally Fowler's takes its name, was more style than substance, Sally's pack has standards that uphold the truth. The film's defender of appearance seems to have strayed too far: the invention of the detachable collar makes evening wear "look better," but Nick's invention of Polly Perkins, which makes von Sloneker look bad, makes Nick look even worse.

On the other hand, appearances can deceive. When Nick presents the story of Polly Perkins, Cynthia (Isabel Gillies) defends von Sloneker, claiming that she knew Polly and it wasn't Rick's fault. Because there is no one Polly Perkins, Cynthia's response proves, Nick argues, "that von Sloneker is doing those kinds of things all the time." The film's exploration of the question of truth emerges in other ways as well.

At one afterparty, Sally Fowler (Dylan Hundley) proposes the game "Truth," in which players answer questions with "absolute honesty and openness." Audrey objects that "there are good reasons why people don't go around telling each other their most intimate thoughts" and that is why there are "convention[s]," but Cynthia accuses her of having something "to hide." Audrey, the reader of Jane Austen, is overruled in her reluctance to play "Truth," and the game proceeds. But we might ask, with whom does Stillman side? In this instance, not only are two players, Jane (Allison Parisi) and Audrey, hurt by "truths" that others reveal, it is not clear that a simple answer to a question can really reveal the truth in all its complexity. When Cynthia reveals the "truth" that the last person she slept with was Nick, for example, its meaning is open to various interpretations, as the subsequent discussion demonstrates.

As to Tom's declaration of his crush on Serena Slocum (Elizabeth Thompson) and his lack of interest in anyone else, events prove that Tom, for all his honesty, was far from understanding his real feelings. The strictures on excessive candor may not be "just a social convention," as Cynthia insists, or even a prudent response to an awareness that the truth may hurt, as Audrey realizes, but a recognition that the truth may not be so simple a matter that it emerges with mere "honesty and openness."

It is Cynthia's ready acceptance of Nick's fabrication about Polly Perkins, after all, that Nick takes as proof that his fabrication was indeed a composite. And what looks like hypocrisy to Nick's accusers (his answering "yes and no," when asked if he made it all up) is in fact the truth, even if Nick's friends do not understand it, and even if Nick may be faulted for applying the device of poetry too simply to life. To say, as Nick does, that *New York Magazine* also creates composites is no justification. Poetry's composites do not speak about individuals, as Nick's does about von Sloneker.

As Christmas vacation approaches its close, the group dissolves. Curiously, it is the initially critical newcomer Tom who seems most distressed. He has also come to appreciate Jane Austen, for now he is actually reading her rather than getting her secondhand through literary critics. He even wonders if "Fourier was a crank." Lest we suppose that the social critic has been co-opted by the system he criticized, we should note that Tom is less concerned by the disintegration of the Rat Pack than by the disappearance of Audrey, for a date with his idealized Serena has opened his eyes to his affection for Audrey. He is even more distraught when he discovers that she has gone with Cynthia to von Sloneker's house party in Southampton and thinks that she may have "turned her back on [Austen]." He and Charlie go on a rescue mission, but of course Audrey's virtue is safe. Von Sloneker is only too glad to have the "flat-chested goody-goody, pain-in-the-neck" leave with her rescuers.

When Nick says good-bye to Tom before heading upstate, he "leave[s] counting on [him] and Charlie to maintain the standards and ideals of the U.H.B.," for "[Tom] and Charlie are the only ones who understand this kind of thing." Although Tom seems perplexed, Nick may again speak the truth, if in fact it takes someone who retains the perspective of the outsider to appreciate and maintain a society's standards and ideals. As they leave von Sloneker's, Audrey asks Tom if he really thinks she is flat-chested. Tom has learned something about excessive candor, or about U.H.B. ideals as well as behavior, for he answers, "Well, I shouldn't say that. The thing is, you look great—and that's what's important. You don't want to overdo it." These are the last words of the movie, and we witness "a small thing, but symbolically important," words that might apply to Stillman's film itself.

Barcelona revolves around two young Americans in Spain and the women they meet, date, and love. Ted Boynton is a sales manager for the Barcelona office of the Illinois High-Speed Motor Corporation, and his cousin Fred is a naval lieutenant doing diplomatic work there during "the last decade of the Cold War." The relation of the cousins is close, but not without friction. Fred drops in on Ted unannounced and takes his prolonged stay for granted. Fred also thinks his cousin "a prig." We see why. Because the "inordinate concern for physical beauty has wrecked...lives," Ted tells his cousin, he has decided to go out only with "plain or homely women." Fred, definitely interested in meeting "terribly attractive women" in Barcelona, and not at all put off by Ted's description of Spanish girls as "really promiscuous," claims that Ted's idea about homely women is "pathetic" and "crazy." No wonder Ted tells his cousin less than he tells us in a voice-over about his "aspiration...to free romance from the chains of physical beauty and carnality," and about how he reads Old Testament books for "advice on romantic matters." If the character of Ted is a development of the virtuous Audrey (Fred refers to Ted as a "goody-goody," as von Sloneker had Audrey), his virtue, as seen through Fred's eyes, appears ridiculous. It is no wonder that Fred cannot resist confiding in Ted's women friends that Ted "is not at all how he seems"—in fact, Fred tells them, Ted admires the Marquis de Sade, and "under the apparently very normal clothes he's wearing these black leather straps, drawn so taut that while he dances...." No wonder, as well, that Ted fails to appreciate Fred as "the best PR guy [he'll] ever have," and doesn't agree with Fred that he should "get down on his knees and thank God [he has] a cousin who makes up interesting stories about [him]."

Ted looks ridiculous enough even without Fred, as he hides his Bible, filled with yellow Post-it notes, inside a copy of the *Economist* and reads the Holy Writ while swaying to the music of Glenn Miller. Perhaps, however, there is good reason to be circumspect about one's faith in a culture where it can be said matter-of-factly, as one of their "cool" women friends Montserrat (Tushka Bergen) does, that "'all the old gods are dead,'—there is no God. That we know." Montserrat seems quite sympathetic to the discovery made by her Spanish lover Ramon (Pep Munne) that "the idea of physical beauty...is the closest thing that remains to divinity in the modern world."

Apart from religion and sex, the other passion in Ted's life is his work. He is devoted to his job in "sales," which he views as "more than just a job.... It's a culture, a whole way of thinking about experience." Along with the Old Testament, Ted believes in "the genius of Carnegie's theory of human relations." In this film, *How I Raised Myself from Failure to Success in Sales* and *The Effective Executive* have replaced *Mansfield Park* and *Persuasion*. Its moral lesson for sales is Ben Franklin's: "to bluntly tell the truth" about one's product, for honesty is "always safe and best." Stillman may have more elevated examples than Ted about what constitutes "the classic literature of self-improvement," but Ted's honest practice results in more than sales: "many [of his customers] also became [his] friends."

If the old gods are dead, however, Fred's patriotism is not. Fred insists on scratching out insulting anti-American graffiti, even if it takes "paint[ing] the whole wall with a ballpoint pen." He also proudly wears his naval dress uniform—to Ted's chagrin—as he and Ted make the rounds of Barcelona's social scene, although it provokes the outcry of "fascist" from the locals. Anti-American feeling intensifies in the course of the film, culminating in Fred's being shot by terrorists. The last quarter of the movie is dominated by Ted's vigil in the hospital at a comatose Fred's bedside, keeping up a steady stream of one-sided conversation or reading aloud in the hope of bringing Fred back to consciousness.

For all the tension between these cousins—which dates back at least to when they were ten, when Fred, without asking, borrowed and accidently sunk Ted's kayak—their differences are more cosmetic than real. Like Fred, Ted is also a patriot, one who not only defends hamburgers but calls Ramon a liar to his face regarding his anti-American statements. Fred, for his part, is not as liberated from bourgeois ideals as his mockery of Ted might indicate. He is astounded when Marta (Mira Sorvino) expresses the view that wanting to get married is "[thinking] in extremist terms." And he desires to meet "the one [woman] in the world [he] was meant to be with."

By the third day of Fred's unconsciousness, Ted confesses that Fred, the stronger swimmer, may in fact have saved his life by going down in his kayak in his place. Ted speaks honestly, although it puts his own long-held grudge against Fred in a petty light. However much Ted understands his honesty in the style of Ben Franklin, his honesty here comes closer to George Washington's. American virtue may be enlightened self-interest, as Tocqueville said, but it occasionally reaches beyond itself.

At Ted's confession, Fred briefly opens his unbandaged eye. But no more than the words of the novel Ted has been reading to Fred do his words of regret by themselves revive his cousin. Only when Ted gets on his knees to pray, asking God to bring Fred back "to full consciousness" and to forgive his "doubting, vainglory, and unworthiness," does Fred speak. "Oh, give me a break," he responds to Ted's prayer, and turns away. One way or another, Ted's prayer has brought Fred out of his coma. "[Fred's] going to have a complete recovery," the ecstatic Ted proclaims to everyone.

A number of brief scenes conclude the movie, including plans for Ted's promotion and transfer back to Chicago and for his marriage to Greta (Hellena Schmied). Ted met Greta in the hospital, when Aurora (Nuria Badia) brought her along to help read to Fred. Ted is evidently not put off by her beauty, asking why she wasn't in any of Ramon's articles about beautiful women. There is a hint that it takes more than physical beauty to capture Ramon's interest when Greta confides that she "loathes" Ramon and thinks he is "repelente." She also draws sketches of hovering angels.

In the last scene of the movie, set in the United States, Greta is with Ted, Montserrat with Fred, and Aurora has been introduced to Ted's business associate Dickie Taylor. They are grilling hamburgers and hot dogs, and bourgeois life in America has never looked so good, at least to the European women who earlier had contempt for hamburgers and other signs of American "culture." Dickie is perplexed that Aurora keeps smirking about his underwear. Ted, who may even be the cause of her smirk, plays along. He has gained enough distance from himself to become playful, and enough confidence to acknowledge Fred's perspective. Ted has not entirely forsworn the romantic illusions he tried earlier to reject. This does not mean that he is any less accepting of bourgeois life than he was earlier in the film. That rejection the film leaves to Ramon. But Ted makes bourgeois life interesting through art, just as Stillman does through his film.

*T*he *Last Days of Disco* returns to Manhattan and to preppies who have graduated to jobs in business, publishing, and law. They frequent an exclusive Manhattan disco club—a place they "always dreamed of. Cocktails, dancing, conversation, exchanges of ideas and points of view. Everyone's here." Little, however, is as it seems in *Last Days*. Charlotte (Kate Beckinsale) and Alice (Chloë Sevigny), who attended college together and now work in the same publishing firm, turn out not to be the friends they seem. Nor is club manager Des (Chris Eigeman) the homosexual he claims to be in order to extricate himself from affairs with women. And the "clients" whom Jimmy Steinway (Mackenzie Astin) gets into the Club through his friendship with Des turn out to be federal investigators. The Club itself, and its culture, encourages the cultivation of appearance: Alice suggests that she and Charlotte will be more likely to get into the Club if they arrive in a cab rather than on foot. Jimmy tries to hide his boss's garish clothes under his own stylish overcoat so that he will more likely be admitted. Tom (Robert Sean Leonard) advises Josh (Matt Keeslar) to "try to avoid eye contact" with the doorman as they go by. Whereas Fred's naval uniform in *Barcelona* is not a costume, even if Marta understands it that way, Des gives his friends costumes to sneak into the Club unknown. Other patrons dress as the Cowardly Lion and the Tin Man. Before the movie is over, the glitter of the Club gives way to its seamy underside—drug dealing and money laundering—followed by arrests and prosecutions.

As in Stillman's other films, *Last Days* has its virtuous heroine. Alice reads, and she has better judgment and more refined tastes than some of her contemporaries. But her hero is J. D. Salinger rather than Jane Austen. She is also plagued with self-doubts and tempted by the experience with men that she lacks. Alice is weaker than *Metropolitan's* Audrey, lacks her moral resources, and is burdened by the advice of Charlotte, who feeds her insecurities under the guise of building her self-esteem. "For most guys, sexual repressiveness is a turnoff," Charlotte confides. But when Alice succeeds in getting Tom into bed, she also loses his respect. Like the Club itself for so many, Alice is for Tom a vision or ideal that disappoints. Unlike the Club, however, Alice suffers, learns, and matures.

In spite of her susceptibility to Charlotte's advice and pressure, Alice makes two choices in the course of the movie that demonstrate her developing strength of character. She accepts Josh, despite his manic depression and Charlotte's contempt for him as a "sicko." Alice also supports the publication of a manuscript on Tibetan Buddhism that Charlotte recommended rejecting. When the author turns out to be a fraud—a writer from Los Angeles rather than the brother of the Dalai Lama he claimed to be, she is able to save "a really good book" by transferring it from "nonfiction" to the "self-actualization" category. Alice's ability to appreciate the virtue in what others find defective reaps her a promotion to associate editor by the end of the film, whereas Charlotte is laid off. Charlotte of course is hardly crushed, for she has no "devotion to the written word" and thinks she will find "a better job in television,...where [her] interests really lie."

Whereas Alice finds worth in a rejected manuscript, Josh criticizes the moral effect of a movie. *Lady and the Tramp* is "a primer for love and marriage directed at very young people, imprinting on their little psyches the idea that smooth talking delinquents recently escaped from the local pound are a good match for nice girls from sheltered homes." The cartoon "program[s] women to adore jerks." The only sympathetic character, the little Scottie who is loyal and concerned about Lady, "is mocked as old-fashioned and irrelevant." Josh not only knows the moral danger of art, he would be able to appreciate Jane Austen. And we have seen his attraction to Alice from the moment he is introduced into the movie.

As assistant district attorney, Josh pursues the arrests and indictments that lead to the demise of the Club he loves. He also warns Des to clean up his act (he is taking cocaine) before the D.A.'s office moves against the Club. In spite of the success of the prosecutions, Josh is laid off for giving "preferential treatment to a friend." He appears to have no regrets, although he must also have that friend's passport confiscated at the airport to force him to do the right thing, to stay to testify. Des for his part is trying to run away, he admits, "like a rat," aware that the "Shakespearean admonition, 'To thine own self be true'" cannot apply to him, for his own self is "pretty bad." Integrity alone is not enough; there are standards by which to measure integrity. It is fitting that he and Charlotte in the end form a couple, as do Josh and Alice. Both couples violate Charlotte's earlier stricture against "ferocious pairing off" from the group, a stricture Charlotte had deployed to keep Alice away from Jimmy until she could grab him for herself. Like integrity, pairing off is not simply good in itself. Pairing off cannot be judged apart from the character of the pair.

Religion makes an appearance in *Last Days* in a more muted form than in *Barcelona*, where there is mention of the Bible, prayer, and angels. Nor does religion receive the serious attention it does in *Metropolitan*, when Charlie argues at an afterparty that most of us as we mature lose our innate belief in God, which we later "regain only by a conscious act of faith"—although Charlie has not yet experienced such an act himself. We do see Charlie's utter faith in Audrey by the end of *Metropolitan*, perhaps foreshadowing *Last Days*. There, Alice not only finds value in a religious book and promotes its publication, she overcomes her hesitancy about Josh,

tually love Audrey was a precondition for his liking Austen. Stillman's films, including the one in which we too meet Audrey, function for us as Audrey does for Tom. Appreciating Austen—or Stillman—is a metaphor for something important today: attaining a comic standpoint of mocking affection rather than of ridicule and cynicism. Ramon, we have seen, attempts to remind his readers of divinity through his stories and photographs of women of extraordinary physical beauty. Stillman suggests that Ramon has had some success; at least he has a following who, whenever we see him, is listening intently. Stillman's films are a better version of Ramon's journalism, for they reveal an inner beauty that reminds us of our connection with something higher than ourselves. We may be laughable, but we are not contemptible. "Mocking affection" fits, even for the bourgeoisie.

In *Metropolitan*, Charlie says that when he first heard of Buñuel's *Discreet Charm of the Bourgeoisie* he "thought, 'finally someone's going to tell the truth about the bourgeoisie,'" but it is "hard to imagine a less fair or accurate portrait." Giving a more fair and accurate portrait—"the bourgeoisie does have a lot of charm," Charlie insists—is presumably how Stillman understands his task. But the task is a difficult one for an artist, not only because like the old gods the bourgeoisie has been discredited, but also because the bourgeoisie has been discredited for being prosaic, charmless. If Stillman shows the charm of the bourgeoisie, as critics recognize, perhaps he can make the old gods credible as well. He does so in part by incorporating into his movies the doubts of even those who believe, as well as criticisms, such as Fred's criticism of Ted's search for a homely woman to marry in *Barcelona*, or Tom's of debutante parties in *Metropolitan*, or even Josh's criticism of himself in *The Last Days of Disco*. And then Stillman shows life triumphing over those doubts and criticisms.

Last Days ends when Josh and Alice meet on the subway on their
way to an exclusive midtown restaurant to celebrate Alice's promotion to associate editor. At the sound of disco music coming
from we know not where, Josh and Alice spontaneously start dancing, and soon everyone in the subway car, and even everyone on
the platform waiting for the train, is dancing—rich and poor, young
and old. Like the vision Stillman captures in his film, the joy from
the music spreads from the couple, not only to those admitted to
an exclusive club, but to everyone. Stillman ends, however, like
Josh before him, on a note of self-mockery, for the disco music
blends into the words of "Amazing Grace." Maintaining through
the end the distance from his film that preserves its charm, Stillman
allows the hymn-singing Charlotte to deliver his film's final message.

Earlier in *Last Days*, the publishing staff where Alice and Charlotte work discuss an outline for how to write a best-seller: "create
sympathetic characters with whom readers identify, give them problems, make those problems big." One member of the staff is disgusted, finds the outline "completely formulaic," and prefers nonfiction to fiction. Stillman, of course, opts for fiction, but he creates
characters who evoke our laughter as well as our sympathy. And
while he gives them problems, it is to his credit that he never makes
those problems bigger than they are. Nor are their solutions out of
reach. Such is his comedy of manners.

Two

Whit Stillman's Restorative Irony

Lauren Weiner

THE CLASSICIST James Alexander Kerr Thomson wrote that "irony, which is a criticism of life, is as hard to define as poetry." The irony that fills the comedies of Whit Stillman actually might not be hard to define—except that the very act of pinning it down is likely to puncture it and let out all the delicate buoyancy. Stillman's film trilogy, *Metropolitan*, *Barcelona*, and *The Last Days of Disco*, and the less accomplished but interesting novelization he wrote of *Last Days*, strongly attract the analyst of culture because the material is so unabashedly bookish and liberal-artsy. Succumbing to the urge to analyze, and aware that I run the risk of investigating away all the charm of these works, I will attempt to look closely at the "criticism of life" offered by this highly entertaining screenwriter-director.

Perhaps the least obtrusive way of beginning is to point to what Stillman evidently thinks is *not* irony, or not a good use of it anyway. Two examples will serve. One is from the novelization, which is entitled *The Last Days of Disco, With Cocktails at Petrossian Af-*

terwards (2000). The film character who in effect steps off the screen to narrate this novel, Jimmy Steinway, declares that he "hate[s] facile-cynical 'ironic' sayings" that are "always being cited by 'knowing' idiots." The second comes from the movie *Barcelona*, where a young sales executive who has taken to heart the writings of Dale Carnegie and other apostles of American business success confides to the viewer in a voice-over that "the enthusiastic, unsophisticated tone of much of this literature did open it up to the facile ridicule of half-wits." It is facile to ridicule the enthusiasms or beliefs of others. It is "irony" with quotes around it—that is, not truly or effectively ironic—to strike a cynical pose toward those conventions and institutions that decent people respect.

We've all seen enough *fin de siècle* situation comedies and *Simpsons* episodes to know that irony is pop culture's tool of choice to debunk tradition or convention. Stillman turns the tables by debunking the debunkers. The criticism he lodges in his literate, hip movies is not aimed at the world at large so much as it is aimed at the very tastes and political and moral valuations of the people who pride themselves on going to literate, hip movies. And his touch is so light that such people apparently don't know what has hit them. The Motion Picture Academy nominated *Metropolitan* for a screenwriting Oscar and *Barcelona* won accolades at the Cannes Film Festival.

In an interview with National Public Radio's Terry Gross in 1998 Stillman explained that his family is of old East Coast lineage and left-wing, Democratic Party sympathies. In his youth he accidentally found himself among a crowd he'd been taught to detest: Manhattan's young debutantes and their escorts, who attended balls in formal wear during "the social season." He was surprised at how nice they were.

Metropolitan is the fruit of his surprise. His film alter ego is

Tom Townsend, Ivy Leaguer and committed socialist, who has been disinherited upon his parents' divorce and who samples this social scene—he claims—out of academic curiosity. Actually, he's lonely and penniless, and he could use the companionship and the free food available at these gatherings.

After the first cotillion, Tom makes as if to extricate himself from his role as one of the male protectors of these debs not yet old enough to have had their coming out. He has told his new acquaintances—they call themselves the Sally Fowler Rat Pack, or SFRP—that he is a student of the writings of Thorstein Veblen and a devotee of the communal model developed by the nineteenth-century French thinker, Charles Fourier. Calmly and gravely he tells the SFRP: "I think it is justifiable to go once, to know at first hand what it is you oppose. I'd read Veblen, but it was amazing to see that these things still go on."

Just as gravely, on the other side of the political spectrum, escort Charlie Black spends these gatherings expressing to his friends his distress at the contempt regularly heaped upon his and their class, the bourgeoisie, "which is responsible for,...well, for nearly everything good that's happened in the last four centuries." He says that he went to see the Luis Buñuel film *The Discreet Charm of the Bourgeoisie* hopeful of a rectification but was shocked at what he saw: "It would be hard to imagine a less fair or accurate portrait."

Charlie takes an immediate dislike to Tom, informing him that "it's untenable" for "someone to say they're morally opposed to deb parties and then attend them anyway." But the two wind up being friends (despite their eventual romantic focus on the same deb, Audrey Rouget, the highly Austenian heroine of the piece). Both young men are guileless and solemn and therefore amusing to viewers. We laugh at their taking themselves so seriously, but at the same time we can't help liking them for doing so. As the barbershop quartet in *The Music Man* asked rhetorically, and so plain-tively: "How can there be any sin in sincere?" In Whit Stillman's world, there can't; sincerity may be the cardinal virtue in his moral universe.

That is why there is not simply sauciness but a dash of real courtesy in SFRP member Jane Clarke's invitation to Tom over the telephone. Jane wants him to don his rented tuxedo for another evening of escort duty, and the clincher is supposed to be, if not the fact that he'll be escorting Audrey Rouget, then that "the party should be of some sociological interest." Jane's wit carries a subtle mixture of elements: it is pointed, playful, but also backhandedly respectful of the way Tom has represented himself before the group. (There is the same mannerly twinkle in *Barcelona* when Fred Boynton, coming upon a Spanish woman outfitted in stunning fifteenth-century garb, extends his hand and says, "I don't think we've met. You're a royal personage of some kind?")

In short, the best ironists in *Metropolitan* are the hyper-conventional members of the SFRP. The least effective ironist is the intellectual radical and outsider, Tom. When Tom tries to pick on these people for their old fogey tastes he is often bested by them— especially by the champion wisecracker, Nick Smith. Tom: "I couldn't believe you were actually going to play bridge. It's such a bourgeois cliché." Nick's lightening-quick response: "That's exactly why I play. I don't enjoy it one bit."

Stillman's special skill is to use comic inflation, first to amuse, but then to subtly effect a reevaluation by us, the audience. After initially considering these formally attired debs and escorts as specimens out of a museum, we gradually begin to take at least a little seriously what they take seriously. When Tom inadvertently loses track of Audrey at the St. Regis Hotel because his head has been turned by an old flame, he is treated like a criminal by members of the SFRP. Audrey has her other companions to fall back on, of course, so their glowering over the abandonment of the damsel comes across as funny—a tempest in a teapot. As the film goes on, though, we find ourselves, if not agreeing with Jane that Audrey has been "totally humiliated" by Tom, then at least hoping along with her that Tom will come to his senses and recognize the attractiveness of this demure, honest, and intelligent creature.

When the cad of the piece, the social titan Rick von Sloneker, shows up at one of the post-cotillion "afterparties," we can measure how far we have come in our Stillman-inspired reevaluation. As Tom did before him, but with a malevolence all his own, von Sloneker slights the very idea of debs and escorts. Whatever we thought of these exotics before, our response to this new attack is not to agree with it but to find the attacker nasty—and a hypocrite to boot, since he preens himself on possessing a European title of nobility.

What is droll is that Tom shelves his objections even more decisively than we do. In his earnest way, and as he accepts the friendship of the SFRP, he takes to being an escort so much that he does not seem to want "the season" to end. The other characters mock him repeatedly for the contradiction between his privileged background (they find out about the trust fund he used to have before his parents' break-up) and his politics. The most piquant teasing of Tom, however, comes in a moment of dramatic irony—in other words, irony generated by the situation itself, not by a character uttering sarcasm. It is in the scene at Grand Central Station where Nick is boarding a train after being ejected from the SFRP for his misbehavior. Upon leaving he designates Tom as the standard-bearer who will replace him. With his traditionalist's sense of symbolism, Nick sanctifies the changing of the guard by making Tom a gift of his shiny black top hat. Now it is the Fourierist who can, in the unlikely event he wants to, stroll down the avenues of the Upper East Side looking like the banker from the *Monopoly* board game.

In trying to capture the understatedness and respectability of these East Coast WASPs and Anglo-Catholics, Stillman has developed a comic style that matches them. He takes the edge off sharp conflicts that arise in his movies. And he takes the edge off sex as well—as we can tell from the title card that flashes on screen to announce what traditionally comes after the official close of the social season. It says: "December 26th, 'Orgy' Week Begins." The ironic quotes around "orgy" are apt: the next shot, accompanied by classical music on the soundtrack, is of the SFRP in a well-appointed apartment at night, fully clothed (in normal jackets, ties, and skirts, not tuxes and ball gowns), with one or two of them thumbing through a book or a magazine as a game of bridge is being set up. Some orgy. Later, to be sure, we do get scenes of co-ed strip poker, drunken tell-all "truth or dare" games, and drug use by Nick and a young woman, Cynthia. But even the drug use is made mild (and therefore funny) when the high-on-mescaline Nick can do nothing but sit and pore over a copy of *Babar*, the classic children's book.

The movie's apostle of gentleness, of course, is Charlie, the "preppy Saint Francis." His morose philosophical disquisitions explore the virtues, but also the defects, of "the whole preppy class"—which he renames, with greater sociological precision, the "urban haute bourgeoisie," giving us yet another new acronym to assimilate (U.H.B.). People "from an uhb background" often fail to hold their own in a society in which achieving upward mobility—or simply maintaining inherited position and wealth—demands personal dynamism. People "from an uhb background" are doomed to downward mobility, complains Charlie, because generations of good manners have rendered them passive.

How fitting that the true U.H.B., Charlie, reacts passively when Tom raises the possibility that the woman they have both come to admire, the virginal Audrey, could be in danger of being taken advantage of by none other than the rich, tall, and menacing Baron Rick von Sloneker. Charlie cannot think the worst because he thinks so highly of Audrey: "She's probably at home asleep right now, with the pink coverlet tucked in tight, and her stuffed animals looking over her." His complacency lasts until Tom, animated by his romantic feelings for Audrey, convinces him that she needs rescuing.

The two travel to Southampton—there is a long scene lampooning their unheroic method of transport, a taxi—and find that Charlie was right. The damsel was not actually in distress. Von Sloneker's activities in his parents' beach house are no worse than the other "orgy" week activities, especially since Audrey, now derided by von Sloneker as a "goody-goody," declined to slip into something more comfortable and he didn't force her to. The subtle irony of the movie's ending is that Charlie's original judgment was correct, but he proves himself an also-ran with this correct judgment, whereas Tom wins the damsel by mistakenly (but admirably) taking the initiative to come and save her.

Nor is it lost on us that this derring-do is performed by someone who, two weeks ago, was a radical critic of bourgeois capitalism and its vestigial aristocratic affectations. In the peculiar Stillmanian way, this character is mocked but also taken at his word, nearly simultaneously. Tom's out-of-step beliefs have been the running joke of the movie. And the running joke peaks just when the movie does. At the faux-chivalric moment of truth, when the good guys (Tom, seconded by Charlie) confront the bad guys (von Sloneker and his sidekick), fisticuffs are on the point of breaking out and Charlie cries: "I warn you, he's a Fourierist!"

This very specific form of U.H.B. humor is on display in *Barcelona* as well. Part of Stillman's charm is the obstinate way his characters have of giving someone or something the benefit of the doubt when it isn't deserved. Charlie in *Metropolitan*, having been introduced to a sleazy record producer, comes away saying: "Maybe underneath it all he's a nice guy. He doesn't make a very good first impression." Similarly, the tone of *Barcelona* is set by Lieutenant Fred Boynton of the U.S. Sixth Fleet. He's a nationalistic hothead— but an uhb-reared one. The sight of him in his Navy uniform prompts murmurs of "facha" ("fascist") and "Yánqui fora" ("Yankee, go home") from passersby in Barcelona's Gothic Quarter. His cousin Ted Boynton, a businessman posted to Spain by his U.S. company, tells him not to take offense because that's what young Spaniards call people just for wearing a coat and tie or for combing their hair. Says Ted: "A military uniform—definitely 'facha.'" Answers Fred: "So 'facha' is something good, then. Because if they were referring to the political movement Benito Mussolini led, I'd be really offended. Men wearing this uniform died ridding Europe of fascism." He is indignant, but his indignation keeps its U.H.B. intonation. Thinking it over: "They obviously didn't mean 'facha' in the positive sense."

While Fred is capable of being offended, others are not. The U.S. Consul in Barcelona, decidedly not a hothead, says that he doesn't think anti-Americanism "is really that significant a phenomenon. It's certainly nothing to take personally." Stillman shows the problem with adopting U.H.B. politeness as a political stance. He has set his movie in the early 1980s, a time of near-confrontation between the Soviet Union and the NATO alliance, and of tension within the Western democracies (the left in Spain, for example, actively opposed Spain's entry into NATO). It begins with an anti-NATO bomb attack against a U.S. target in Barcelona, and the attacks continue throughout—including Fred's serious injury in an assassination attempt. In Stillman's screenplay—but missing from the film—is a scene in which the consul is hunted down and shot by terrorists right after poo-pooing the significance of anti-Americanism—a dramatic irony that raps the high-toned WASP establishment (whose members have staffed the U.S. foreign service since the beginning of the republic) for its appeasement-minded liberalism.

Stillman, as screenwriter, chose an uncharacteristically heavy-handed way to deliver this message. It doesn't seem a terrible loss that Stillman, as director, left out the assault on the consul; what remains in the film conveys his views sufficiently well. The Snidely Whiplash of *Barcelona* is another continental, a real one this time, unlike the wannabe von Sloneker in *Metropolitan*. Ramon, a womanizing Spanish academic-turned-journalist, is the anti-American guru of Barcelona's intellectual class. As one of his acolytes, the beautiful Montserrat, explains: "He had read the works of Philip Agee and so was an expert on the American CIA and its involvement in the internal affairs of every country." Ramon seems to dog the Boyntons' social periphery, constantly holding forth in his corner of a restaurant, café, or party to assorted journalists and graduate student types, as well as to Montserrat and the other "trade-fair girls" whom Ted deals with professionally at Barcelona's trade center. (They are, in a way, the film's "debs.")

According to the Spaniard's Philip Agee-inspired theory, the current rash of terrorism against "los yánquis" in Barcelona is the diabolically clever work of U.S. intelligence. Those ruthlessly cynical U.S. agents, claims Ramon, are trying to stir up anti-terrorist sentiment in the United States before the presidential election as this "might rescue the American president's reclining [sic] popularity." Ted Boynton, who diplomatically does his best to respect local customs and sensitivities, and to avoid controversy, can't help but let loose and tell Ramon off for spreading "disgusting lies" about his country.

The ideological antipathy is compounded—as is often the case in a Stillman plot—by sexual competition. Ramon writes articles about the aesthetics of female beauty and seduces women as part of his "research." Ted, who has begun a romantic involvement with

Montserrat, learns that she has been a kind of concubine of Ramon's since she was sixteen. Ted voices a moral objection to the way she was initiated into sex (although he has no objection to sleeping with her now). Where he is earnest and flat-footed, his cousin Fred finds a devious way to insult Ramon: he spreads a theory of his own. "I think it's well known," Fred says, "that anti-Americanism has its roots in sexual impotence. At least in Europe."

The point-counterpoint that is established, from early on, between Ramon and Ted becomes more piquant the closer one looks. All who are within earshot of Ramon learn how "progressive unionism" in Europe was undermined after World War II by the anticommunist agents of that "powerful North American syndicate," the "AFL-CIA." Cut to Ted, in a *tête-à-tête* with Montserrat. Ted is telling her of his personal hero, the founder of the international firm he works for. His boss Jack Tyrrell is "one of those magnetic personalities from the World War II generation—he was with Wild Bill Donovan in the OSS and parachuted into Sicily before the allied landings." It is as if the CIA's precursor—the OSS—has been brought in immediately as a way of correcting the record. What Ted says, moreover, backs up the point his cousin made in that early scene: it is the much-maligned Americans who have the most unimpeachably anti-"facha" record, in historical terms.

Montserrat and another trade-fair girl, Marta, are much impressed with "the AFL-CIA" and its evil deeds. Ted tries patiently to untangle Ramon's tendentious imprecisions, explaining and defending the American labor movement, describing its Federation of Labor, the merger with the "more militant CIO," etc. His patriotic clarifications, however, produce an extra turn of Stillmanian irony. Ted extols Jay Lovestone and the other "American labor leaders who came to Europe then." Montserrat responds: "So what Marta said is partly true.... I'm sure I've heard of the AFL-CIA. There is some important American labor union of that name."

Those who know their Cold War history are amused, not just at the young woman's Gracie Allen-ish persistence in misunderstanding, but at the subtext. Lovestone's part of the labor movement did indeed involve itself in "internal affairs" in some allied countries to stop European labor unions from going communist. Score one, implicitly, for Ramon. Stillman is forever challenging the prejudices of the *bien pensant* "progressives" by explaining what they leave out and celebrating what they disdain—but sometimes he gives just a little something back to those prejudices.

The same thing can be observed in the movie's treatment of the "culture of sales" to which Ted cleaves so fervently. In an early voice-over—which narrates a montage of images, including an elementary-school production of *Death of a Salesman*—Ted describes himself as a convert to this culture. "I had seen Arthur Miller's play and as a youth had the usual sneering, deprecating attitude to the world of business and sales." His view changed when he had a charismatic business professor in college and then found Jack Tyrrell's firm, IHSMOCO (which stands for the Illinois High Speed Motor Corporation). The classic books of business by "Franklin, Emerson, Carnegie, and Bettger" have become as important to him as any other book—except the Bible, of course, which he only takes out when alone in his apartment and, in the funniest cinematic solo dancing since Tom Cruise in *Risky Business* (1983), reads to himself while jitterbugging to Glenn Miller music.

Ted defends the culture of sales against all comers, including his cousin Fred. Indeed, in the scene where Ted complains about "the facile ridicule of half-wits," Fred is the half-wit in question. He has asked facetiously if "maybe I could use the same self-motivational techniques you use in sales in my Navy career: 'Every day in every way I'm becoming a better and better lieutenant junior grade'...." Icily Ted points out that that's autosuggestion, "popularized by Coue during the twenties but totally unserious."

As both cousins become involved with trade-fair girls, Ted employs business principles to resolve his romantic problems. He decides that "Maneuver X" could be his only chance to decisively win Montserrat away from Ramon. Maneuver X means "removing all pressure, creating a sort of space which the customer must affirmatively cross." Fred is struck, for once, by his businessman-cousin's wisdom: "Wow. You've really thought this through. That's impressive. I haven't thought through anything about Marta.... But—isn't Maneuver X really just another way of putting what we usually refer to as 'playing hard to get'?" Ted: "No." Fred: "Huhn."

What we have is, once again, the defense of the bourgeois and the American, but with Stillman giving a little bit back to the prejudices of the bourgeois-haters. Some business concepts surely are—whether businessmen will admit it or not—insubstantial claptrap, or simply disguised truisms. What still stands, I think, is the film's endorsement of the sweetly reverent moment in which Ted reads aloud to a Spanish colleague from one of his Franklinesque texts: "The wisest and best salesman is always the one who bluntly tells the truth about his article.... If he does not sell the first time, he leaves a trail of trust behind. Being bluntly honest is always safe and best." This nugget of truth has done more to promote the culture of democracy internationally than the ideas of "progressives" like Arthur Miller ever have.

At the film's end, Ramon seeks out Lieutenant Boynton and apologizes for having written the newspaper article about him that made him a target for violence. But even with this smoothing over of a personal conflict—a typical Stillmanian no-hard-feelings-old-man sort of moment—the triumph of the American Way could not be more mischievously complete, as the movie fades on Ted and Fred, back in the good old U.S. of A., plying their new Spanish wives with hamburgers hot off the backyard grill.

In his 1998 interview with Terry Gross, Stillman explained that, although the rarified world of escorts and debs had involved formal role-playing, there was little sexual pressure associated with assuming those roles. It was the young women who extended the invitations; the young men who accompanied them were not actually taking the debs on a date. Both gained valuable experience in being around the opposite sex without the expectation of even a goodnight kiss. The formality of it all—and the fact that it was group socializing—could be surprisingly liberating to the awkward and sensitive adolescent, according to the filmmaker.

The Last Days of Disco depicts the same sort of people as they've gotten slightly older, and the sexual pressure is now extreme. Stillman uses his comic gift this time to commend to us what was good about the vanished world of disco decadence. As he explained to Gross, there was group socializing inside Manhattan's "red velvet rope clubs," just as there had been at the debutante balls. Discos—so maligned at the time by avant-garde intellectuals—were an oasis in the social wasteland of an era in which it was oh-so-fashionable to deride cocktail parties. "Clubs are a good thing, not a bad thing," said Stillman, sounding very much like one of his characters.

The disco-goers in the movie, which takes place in the very early 1980s, face a daunting prospect in getting past the heavily guarded red velvet rope and into "the Club." Only one character complains about the gauntlet of exclusivity *per se,* and even he, an underpaid editorial assistant of anti-elitist, anti-bourgeois sensibilities, is thrilled to get in. Stillman's spokesman on this matter is a Harvard graduate and assistant district attorney, Josh Neff, who considers himself—despite seldom gaining admittance to the Club—"a loyal adherent to the Disco Movement." For Josh, disco is what he has "always dreamed of—cocktails, dancing, conversation, the exchange of ideas and points of view." Or, as the beautiful and delightfully bad Charlotte Pingree puts it: "It's really important there be more group social life. Not just all this ferocious pairing off." Charlotte isn't being sincere in that particular remark, of course. She pairs off quite ferociously, especially when by doing so she can show up Alice Kinnon, the movie's heroine and supposedly her closest female friend, by stealing Alice's prospective love interest.

Josh and Charlotte are given, separately, long speeches early in the movie that start us out on very contrasting notes. His is pure, Stillman-style Pollyanna. Hers reeks of cynicism about the world and about how to win in the battle of the sexes. He speaks of the glamour and excitement of group socializing and even makes a case for the "up-tempo Philadelphia international hits" that started the dance-music craze: "Some people don't consider that disco because it's good, but I remember feeling absolutely electrified."

Where Josh is humble, Charlotte is hubristic. She assumes she will be selected from the crowd out front of the Club and she is—on her first try. She is with Alice, her quieter, more intelligent friend from college, and as the two enter the hallowed precincts she treats Alice to a lecture on the advent of new and advantageous sexual *mores*. Alice is sweet, politely candid, and intellectually (though not sexually) self-confident. Charlotte is her opposite, a font of lies, catty insults, and feminist bromides: "I just think it's so important to be in control of your own destiny, not to fall into that fifties cliché of waiting for guys to call. The right ones never do. The ones who do, you have to make the most ridiculous excuses to. The nice ones get hurt feelings and hate you, the jerks inevitably corner you into going out anyway.... Thank God this is a whole new era of music and social models. We're in complete control."

Of course they will find out differently. The main way that the irony develops here is in the testing and distorting of the scruples of Alice, for which Charlotte—who is Thackeray's Becky Sharp against a *Looking for Mr. Goodbar* backdrop—is largely responsible. Alice is not in control at all. She is on a professional and romantic roller coaster, the latter being almost entirely of Charlotte's making. Charlotte, who cons Alice into rooming with her, breaks it to Alice that "there's something of the kindergarten teacher in you." This can be overcome, however: "Throw the word 'sexy' into your conversation. It's kind of a signal."

In implementing Charlotte's antidote to nerdiness, Alice becomes much like the unwitting Ted Boynton in *Barcelona*. His smart-alecky cousin Fred had tried to enhance Ted's profile with the opposite sex by claiming that staid-looking Ted wore the leather gear of a sadist under his business suit. In that case, the intended targets (the trade-fair girls) were drawn in until Ted angrily disproved Fred—by going into the restroom with Montserrat and revealing normal BVDs. In Alice's case, the nerd in question goes along willingly. An eligible-seeming environmental lawyer, Tom Platt, is drawn in—but only long enough for a drunken one-night stand with Alice at his apartment. The excruciatingly funny payoff to Charlotte's meddling comes the next time Platt sees Alice. A regretful Platt confides that "what I was *craving* was the sort of sentient individual who wouldn't abandon her intelligence to hop in bed with every jerk she meets at a nightclub.... Please don't tell me that's not slutty." He ends his outburst by saying that what really galls him, in retrospect, is the affected way she slinked around his apartment, calling his comic book collection "sexy." "Uncle Scrooge is *sexy*?! My God, is there no limit?!"

At the next meeting things get worse still. Alice tells Platt she had come to him a virgin, and this paragon of an environmental lawyer reveals to her that he, in effect, has spread epidemiological pollution. He has given our heroine two sexually transmitted diseases. Charlotte, suspecting Alice has gonorrhea but not realizing she also has herpes, which is "serious" because not curable, tells her protégée to look on the bright side, "Everyone gets something," she says, speaking from experience. And anyway, "VD's not all bad"—you have to look up all your old lovers to let them know they might be infected, and some of these reunions may well turn into satisfying romantic interludes. For all the frothy wit and *élan* of this movie, it is, from this moment on, tinged with portents of the historical moment and hence, with sadness. When Jimmy Steinway, the junior ad executive who spends the whole movie trying to get his clients into the Club, voices his sense of foreboding and predicts that "a meteorite is headed straight for it," he is pointing not only to the coming death of a fad but to the death—from a disease that has yet to announce itself—of many of the gay revelers depicted here.

The sadder but wiser Alice gradually attracts the active romantic interest of Jimmy and every other male member of this U.H.B. social circle. She does so after her affliction becomes known, so Stillman would clearly like us to believe it plausible that the men's attitude is as *blasé* as Charlotte's. Honest Alice pulls well ahead of manipulative Charlotte in the popularity sweepstakes, thus keeping in play—STD or no STD—the traditional question at the heart of any romantic comedy: whom will our heroine choose? One new suitor is, in fact, drawn to Alice precisely because she has contracted a "social disease": the Club's assistant manager, Des McGrath, a former Harvard classmate of Jimmy, Josh, and Tom Platt who sometimes helps them get into the Club. The cocaine-snorting, womanizing Des now feels Alice is "not operating on a plane so far removed from the rest of us.... There's hope for me." Well, Charlotte had said that if Alice loosened up new opportunities would arise for her, and so they have.

The Last Days of Disco contains little discussion of what makes a woman worthy of love. Dwelling upon the subject of maidenly purity would not, after all, be apt given the direction things have taken. But there is much discussion of what makes a man worthy of love. All such talk is cleverly centered around Josh's exegesis of a classic Disney movie he considers to have had a baneful effect on generations of American girls and women. The 1950s movie *Lady and the Tramp*, he tells Alice and company, has "program[med] women to adore jerks" by "imprinting on their little psyches the idea that smooth-talking delinquents recently escaped from the local pound" make better mates than straight-arrow types, like the little Scottie dog in the movie "who's so concerned about Lady" but who is "mocked as old-fashioned...and shunted off to the side."

The Baby Boomers' total seriousness about the profundity of popular culture is being made fun of here. It is also being put to good use—both as Josh's unsubtle way of enjoining Alice to choose him and not Des, and as a reinforcement of Charlotte's early pronouncement on sexual politics. ("The nice ones get hurt feelings.... The jerks inevitably corner you into going out anyway.") Our rakish "Tramp," Des, understands this move and strikes back at the "Scottie dog," Josh, throwing up to him—in front of "Lady"—the fact that his old schoolmates know he is manic depressive. (Josh later assures Alice that he controls his condition by taking lithium, "a naturally occurring salt.")

The surprising surge of Josh as a candidate for Alice's affections parallels his emergence as the rod of justice that must sweep down upon his beloved disco to stop the drug-dealing and money-laundering going on behind the dancing and the strobe lights. As assistant district attorney, he is in on the accelerating criminal investigation, and he gives his rival Des fair warning to stop using or passing on cocaine lest he be snared in the dragnet. Des finds to his dismay that another of the circle of friends—his best friend, in fact, Jimmy—has also been in on the investigation, cooperatively ushering advertising clients into the Club who were really undercover G-men gathering criminal evidence.

In the novelization of *The Last Days of Disco* the narrator, Jimmy Steinway, is presented as a pilgrim in the same faith as Josh. Jimmy says (hitting the point rather ploddingly, as is unfortunately often the case in the novel version): "It was 'ironic' I suppose that the two of us most in thrall to the Club...should be those who played the most visible role in its undoing." The much more piquant irony here is that Des's unsavory and pony-tailed boss, the Wiseguy-esque yet countercultural Bernie, had a well-developed prejudice against Des's U.H.B. friends, particularly those in advertising. He had been loath to let "that element" into his chic establishment—above all, because they are *nice*. Now that he is about to get busted by ad-men who were really G-men, his anti-bourgeois prejudice is borne out in a way that he (and we) would never have predicted. He is led away in handcuffs and his disco is headed for closing.

Consider, for a moment, what is *not* in the film's denouement. No one expresses disapproval of Josh's law-and-order zeal having spoiled the fun. Des McGrath is angry; but we see him directing most of his ire at his best friend Jimmy, who has betrayed him. As Jimmy explains, "There's a higher loyalty." The message: being a narc, while by no means pleasant, is sometimes the right thing to do. No one fusses against accepting this—not even the "Tramp," when all is said and done. Josh pleads with Des to do his part and testify in court against Bernie instead of, "out of selfishness or in-difference or a kind of fashionable cynicism," merely looking the other way. Des first tries to skip the country but, in a final twist, we catch up with him back in Manhattan. He'd been prevented from leaving and has given evidence against his crooked boss. He tells Josh: "I'm glad I stayed." He doesn't even really mind losing Alice to Josh, since he and the equally rascally Charlotte take up the film's last frames deciding what a great pair they would make.

The novelization contains an interesting phrase from Alexander Pope's *Essay on Man*: "Whatever is, is right." Pope's words are immediately challenged by the narrator. Yet they encapsulate nicely the goal pursued by Stillman: to depict another "misrepresented and sneered at" phenomenon of middle-class American existence—disco—as a partly good thing that, for partly very good reasons, had to cease to be. Stillman accepts what is. He shows himself eager to overcome the knee-jerk bohemian's critique of the matter at hand but less prepared to swat down the objections of mainstream morality.

A sincerity that doubles back—this is the special ironic effect for which Stillman strives. As Josh says in the sermon that closes *The Last Days of Disco*—with his friends conscientiously hanging on his words, and bells chiming in the background as an audience-nudging accent of ersatz loftiness—disco will for a time "be considered passé and ridiculous," will be laughed at and derided, but it is "too great and too much fun to be gone forever. It's got to come back some day. I just hope it will be in our own lifetimes. [Pause] Sorry. I've got a job interview this afternoon and I was trying to get revved up. But most of what I said I—uh—believe."

Three

WHIT STILLMAN:
POET OF THE BROKEN BRANCHES

James Bowman

IT IS A MISTAKE, I think, to look at Whit Stillman as an apologist for what one of his characters in *Metropolitan* wanted to call the urban haute bourgeoisie, or U.H.B. Apart from anything else, it is far from clear whether any such thing actually exists in nature in the form proposed by the term's inventor, Charlie Black. To Charlie, it seems to mean the same thing as WASPs, "preppies," or "People Like Us," but with the vague expectation that the quasi-academic, quasi-sociological sound of "urban haute bourgeoisie" will prevent it from accruing the connotations of racialism or snobbery which attach to the older terms. Yet there are plenty of people from any sociologically identifiable equivalent of the urban haute bourgeoisie, even those who have lived all their lives on the Upper East Side of Manhattan, who nevertheless would see the characters in *Metropolitan* as being quite as alien as they appear to most Americans.

This nonexistence of Charlie and his friends as an identifiable social sub-class in the real world is surely the point about them in the movie. It may be that there are in New York (or were, as late as the 1980s) young people of twenty or so who still go to deb parties in white tie and tails, seem to have no interest in rock 'n' roll or much popular culture subsequent to the 1950s, and whose social chit-chat is sprinkled with references to Thorstein Veblen, Lionel Trilling, and Jane Austen. But the rarity of such creatures and the ideal quality of their world is something that Stillman's characters themselves seem to assume. In Charlie's case, that assumption is what lies behind his prophecies of impending preppy doom. In *Metropolitan*, what binds these characters together is not social class, or money, or even their shared prep school backgrounds, so much as the fact that they are all young people who have taken up in one way or another an implicitly adversarial relationship to the youth culture whose values predominate among their coevals.

True, the contrast between the culture of these *rara aves* and that of their more recognizable contemporaries is mostly implicit. The big dogs of the 1980s pop scene are the barkless canines of Stillman's film whose absence helps to define in outline what a notional alternative to their cultural tyranny might look like. For Stillman's real purpose in inventing such outlandish characters as Charlie and Tom Townsend and Nick Smith and Audrey Rouget is not to defend some notional class of juveniles who are still prepared to argue the merits of the detachable collared shirt—as opposed to the soft-collared—so much as it is to call such a class into existence.

Whether or not, that is, these people actually exist, they are so rare that it is as if they didn't. Stillman is perhaps trying to disguise his and their isolation from the depressing realities of late-twentieth-century America by putting the phantom class of the U.H.B. on a par with other categories called into existence by sociological nominalists. But his subsequent films, *Barcelona* and *The Last Days of Disco*, make it clear that their real function is to give us a hard but not unhopeful look at the prospects for innocence in our time. By this I mean not just, or perhaps not even, sexual innocence. His characters all live in the ever-widening wake of the sexual revolution and are not politically or spiritually self-confident enough to set themselves up as ideologically motivated opponents of that revolution in the way that subsequently young people have done in *True Love Waits* and the pro-virginity movement. But regret for lost innocence of a more general kind is such a recurring theme for Stillman that his literary forebears would seem to be Alain-Fournier and J. D. Salinger.

In part this is the merely sentimental innocence of those from well-to-do families who have enjoyed sheltered childhoods. But the note of nostalgia—sometimes for a world that they themselves have never known—is seldom struck by his young characters without also making the serious point that they are bewildered by what it means to be an adult in a culture dominated by the values of children. Their nostalgia for childhood is also a paradoxical longing to be shown the way out of childhood by parents who want to be children themselves. Tom and Nick in *Metropolitan* discover a box of toys put out in the street for the trash collector. "The childhood of our whole generation is represented here, and they're just throwing it out," laments Nick. But the more particular and poignant significance of the box only becomes clear with Tom's realization that the toys are his own, and they are being thrown out by his divorced and remarried father, who has left town without telling him.

This too is characteristic in Stillman's work. The childhood innocence of which the film is so solicitous is continually under assault from the selfishness and sexual self-indulgence of the previous generation. It is this harder but usually hidden edge to his satire which saves Stillman from a J. M. Barrie-like idealization of childish innocence. His characters' reminiscences about the past always have a purpose in making the present appear more clearly defined in its foolishness, wrong-headedness, or backwardness by contrast. Thus Josh in *The Last Days of Disco* is remembered by the other characters, especially Des, as having stood on a table and sung the hymn by John Greenleaf Whittier which begins, "Dear Lord and Father of Mankind, forgive our foolish ways." He had to leave college for a while.

To Des, who left Harvard for more conventional reasons, this was the defining moment of Josh's life, though Josh himself is now inclined to play it down. He was treated for depression and is now "normal." Yet as he gingerly explores the feelings of Alice on the subject of his breakdown, Josh shows that he has forgotten none of the words to the hymn:

> Breathe through the heats of our desire
> Thy coolness and thy balm.
> Let sense be dumb, let flesh retire,
> Speak through the earthquake, wind, and fire
> O still small voice of calm.

Whether Alice is genuinely alarmed by the evidence of an unbalanced personality provided by Josh's impromptu recitation of these healing and comforting words or whether she only pretends to be, it is clearly Whit Stillman's excellent joke about a popular culture so heated by "our desire" that a longing for coolness and balm is seen as a sign of madness.

This scene also furnishes a clue as to what it is that prevents his idealization of the past from degenerating into mere nostalgia. For whether it is represented by Glenn Miller in *Barcelona*, or by the hymns in *Metropolitan* and *Last Days*, or by the disco music of the latter, the idealized past nearly always stands for a much less subjective and more accessible kind of goodness and innocence. In *Barcelona*, for example, the lost ideal is political innocence, in the sense of a belief in the essential benevolence of American power in the world—which was becoming as rare or rarer than sexual innocence by the early 1980s when the film is set. The belief in love, friendship, and the American world-imperium all come together in that film as part of a complex which Stillman presents to us as a bulwark against the prevailing cynicism. This he does in the same spirit of gentle self-deflation with which Nick offers his defense of preppy-culture and Josh offers his of disco-culture—that is, with assurances that they believe at least *some* of what they say.

In some ways, *Barcelona* is the most ambitious of the three films. It presents us with two American archetypes: Ted Boynton and his cousin Fred, the one an earnest, upright, hard-working Puritan and the other an irreverent, iconoclastic, good-time guy. Both of them have to come to terms with a culture which is at best bewildered by and at worst hostile to all that they take for granted about the world. Ted's virtue and belief in Dale-Carnegieism is mocked and disparaged while Fred's irreverence comes up against the new pieties of what we now call "political correctness." The hostility that both encounter from the ambient culture of post-Franco Spain is what brings the two together again after an almost inevitable estrangement, uniting all that Stillman sees as being best about America.

There is a marvelous scene early in this film in which Fred tells some of the remarkably pretty but "promiscuous" girls of Barcelona that his cousin "might seem like a typical American, like a big, unsophisticated child, but he's far more complex than that." Not only is he "an admirer of the Marquis de Sade and a follower of Dr. Johnson" whose nickname is *punta de diamante*, but he wears tight leather thongs under his clothes to give himself a masochistic thrill as he dances. As intended, the girls are impressed, but the joke is on them. Fred takes advantage of their own childish credulity about American childishness to show that they are in fact the "unsophisticated" ones, easily seduced by false tales of perverted sexual practices and psychological "complexity" because the straightforwardness and plain-dealing of Ted as he really is is beyond their comprehension.

Later, Fred defends his lies to Ted by saying, "Do you think any even mildly cool trade fair girl would give you the time of day if she knew the pathetic, Bible-dancing goody-goody you really are?" But he also points to the dilemma that confronts them both when he adds that there are books and movies about sado-masochism. "At least people into S&M have a *tradition!*" he remarks—unlike, that is, the victims of the American cultural shipwreck of the 1970s who are forced to invent their own traditions, perhaps something like Ted's weird practice of dancing (alone) to the music of Glenn Miller while reading the Bible. Likewise, in *The Last Days of Disco*, the young professionals take up the dance craze of the 1970s as heralding (falsely, as it turns out) a return to the courtship rituals of their parents, or even their grandparents.

All these characters constitute not some identifiable urban haute bourgeoisie defined by income, education, or ethnicity, but Stillman's representatives of the orphans of the sexual and, at least partly, political revolutions of the 1960s. Their cause is not the retention of entrenched power or privilege but the right to hold on to customs and beliefs that they persist in believing to be something more than the ideology of a ruling class. For the popular culture has tended to adopt the Marxist-Leninist view of American power as imperialist, just as it has also adopted the weird, Freudian-feminist view of traditional sexual morality and courtship customs as "repressive." More recently it has been picking up academic-Marxist views about the old bourgeois high culture of Dr. Johnson and Jane Austen. Scarcely knowing what they were doing, the carriers of the popular culture have cut a swath through the old culture, throwing up broken branches left and right. Stillman is the poet of the broken branches, of the fragmentary remains of the old, unpoliticized culture which both he and his most articulate characters continue to believe was not what present-day ideologues think it was but what the people who developed it over the centuries thought it was.

In other words, Stillman stands for the right of the past not to be colonized by the present, not to be politicized by what in historical terms is our very parochial tendency to see all things in terms of power distribution. Even when his characters are political, like Tom in *Metropolitan*, their views are likely to be expressed in the most quaint and old-fashioned ways. Tom is a follower of Charles Fourier, the French utopian socialist and author of *Le Nouveau Monde Industriel* who was the inspiration for Brook Farm. When Charlie points out that Brook Farm ceased to exist and therefore Fourierism was a failure, Tom quietly replies: "Everyone ceases to exist; that doesn't mean everyone's a failure." Although Tom abandons his Fourierism by the end of the film, his forlorn clinging to a long-outdated creed is treated with typical respect by Stillman. Later it is Tom himself who has to be put right by Audrey when he tells her that "nearly everything that Jane Austen wrote looks ridiculous from today's perspective."

"Has it ever occurred to you," she replies with her own version of Stillmanian quixotism, "that today from Jane Austen's perspective would look even worse?"

There is an interesting inversion of this remark in *Barcelona*, when Ted observes to Fred that the sexual revolution lately come to post-Franco Spain has turned the world upside down. "Has it ever occurred to you that the world was upside down before and is now right side up?" asks Fred.

"No, I don't think that's it," Ted answers.

In an interview with *Psychology Today*, Whit Stillman spoke of the effect on him of having spent his junior year abroad in Mexico:

> It turned out to do the opposite of what it was supposed to do. It didn't make me a mushroom-dropping pothead; seeing another culture and the way the less affluent in that culture coped with life actually made me much more conventional. It made me more respectful of conventional people in the United States.

He goes on to give this example:

> The people we derided in Cambridge were the Pine Manor [College] girls who wore pink pastels and came in on Saturday nights sort of overdressed. The farm girls in Cuernavaca, Mexico, on Saturday night came in wearing the same colors. No politically correct Harvard person would sneer, because they're working class—and yet their aspirations were so similar to the aspirations of all the people we sneered at back in Cambridge. It makes you think about what it is you should really disrespect.

This is the heart of Whit Stillman's filmmaking purpose. His characters are all ideal versions of himself: kids from privileged backgrounds who learn not to feel guilty or ashamed of the fact. But because there are so few such people in reality, or at least so few who are able to give expression to their uncomplicated identities, we have to take them on trust. They are, as it were, hypothetical. But the people Stillman is really writing for are those just below him on the social scale. Not the urban *haute* bourgeoisie but the suburban *petite* bourgeoisie, who ape their betters even when it amuses their betters to sneer at people like themselves. Stillman instead holds up for their admiration a version of what the upper class—that upper class that the middle classes have always emulated—would be if it existed in our world. And because he does this in a spirit neither of snobbish superiority nor of fashionable self-hatred but of good-humored self-depreciation, he makes of the U.H.B. something genuinely admirable.

New Line Cinema Corp.

Metropolitan (1990)

Four

FROM MANSFIELD TO MANHATTAN: THE ABANDONED GENERATION OF *METROPOLITAN*

R. V. Young

A FEW YEARS AGO, Duke professors William H. Willimon and Thomas H. Naylor, collaborating on an urgent critique of higher education in America, asked this question about the college students of the preceding two decades: "Are we reaping the results of a generation of students abandoned by the previous generation, left to their own devices, having no more textured goal for their lives than to be rendered into efficient, passive machines for the acquisition of money?"

This description fits quite well the youthful characters of Whit Stillman's film, *Metropolitan*, which premiered at the Sundance Film Festival five years before the publication of Willimon and Naylor's book. Parents and other fully mature adults are conspicuously absent from all but a handful of scenes; when they do appear, they are largely ineffectual. As the film opens, for example, Audrey Rouget's mother tries to convince her daughter that her behind is not "enormous," despite the remarks of her younger brother. Although Mrs.

Rouget has some success in providing comfort about the size of Audrey's posterior, she also seems to leave her daughter worrying about the size of her nose. Tom Townsend's mother only manages to provoke her son's annoyance when she reminds him that he must return his rented tuxedo in order to avoid an additional day's charge—he returns it late anyway—and her only success is providing him with money she can ill spare so that he can continue going to the debutante parties which he has affected to despise. Fathers make no appearance in the film, and they seem mainly to be remote figures who have abandoned their families and taken up with sinister stepmothers. *Metropolitan* thus presents a world reminiscent of the *Peanuts* cartoon strip, where youthful figures are left on their own without visible adult guidance or influence. The concern of Willimon and Naylor about the crisis of an "abandoned generation" on campus had already been given cinematographic embodiment by Whit Stillman.

Once this fundamental theme of *Metropolitan* is grasped, its general import becomes clear and its more puzzling details fall into place. The film is a dramatization of young men and women—the main characters all seem to be in their first year of college, eighteen or nineteen years old—who are morally disoriented because they have been left to their own devices by parents who have neglected their traditional duties and absconded into the realm of their own failures, pleasures, and longings. Although these are young persons with a patina of sophistication—the children of affluent families, beneficiaries of expensive prep school educations who inhabit an exclusive milieu of debutante balls and parties in Manhattan—they are not well equipped to cope with the transition from adolescence to adulthood in what amounts to a moral and social vacuum.

The abrupt departure of Nick Smith, whose perspective dominates the first half of the film, is thematically coherent when we recognize that he is attempting to fulfill a role that is beyond his capacity. Likewise, the muted and modest triumph of Audrey Rouget and Tom Townsend at the end is possible because they occupy a place at the margins of the "Sally Fowler Rat Pack." Finally, the meaning of the work is illuminated by observing its analogical relationship to Jane Austen's *Mansfield Park*. Even as *Clueless* is an adaptation of Austen's *Emma*, transposing into a contemporary setting her insights about the ways young women interact with one another as they seek the attentions of men, so *Metropolitan* is a (considerably more subtle) reprise of the great English novelist's account of the moral and spiritual peril encountered by young men and women when their elders fail to exercise proper authority. Stillman's film is not an allegory, not a symbolic rendering of the decline of Western civilization; it is, rather, a generally light-hearted comedy in which the irony is tilted toward wry amusement rather than the mordant satire of *saeva indignatio*. Like Austen's comedy, however, *Metropolitan* has profound moral implications, which are only enhanced by its wit and humor.

The connection with *Mansfield Park* is the best place to begin, since it seems to be a deliberately placed index of the film's ethical orientation. Jane Austen is a favorite of Audrey Rouget. At one point, after Tom Townsend has inadvertently wounded her by leaving her at a party to take Serena Slocum home, Audrey is shown staring at the complete six-volume Oxford edition of Austen in a store window. More important is a conversation between Audrey and Tom about Lionel Trilling's essay on *Mansfield Park*, which reveals a great deal about both characters. It is clear that the sophisticated irony of Trilling's essay has eluded Audrey's practical and virtuous mind:

> I think he's very strange. He says that "nobody" could like the heroine
> of *Mansfield Park*. I like her. Then he goes on and on about how "we"

modern people, today, with "our" modern attitudes "bitterly resent" *Mansfield Park* because its heroine is virtuous. What's wrong with a novel having a virtuous heroine?

Audrey's naïveté about Trilling's critical subtleties is, however, no more mistaken than Tom's brash assurance that the essay condemns as "simply absurd" the "novel's premise—that there's something immoral in a group of young people putting on a play." When he admits that he has not even read Austen's work, it becomes apparent that Tom has considerably less understanding of literature (and literary interpretation) than Audrey:

> I don't read novels. I prefer good literary criticism—that way you get both the novelists' ideas and the critics' thinking. With fiction I can never forget that none of it really happened—that it's all just made up by the author.

While none of these observations will get high marks in English class, what makes this amusing effort at literary discussion significantly ironic is that Tom and Audrey are, to some extent, living out the situation of *Mansfield Park*—it really is happening to them. That Tom and Audrey are themselves fictional creations only adds a self-reflexive element to Stillman's irony.

Mansfield Park is the story of a poor relation, Fanny Price—a shy, bookish, rather plain but good-hearted girl—who falls secretly and, apparently, hopelessly in love with her cousin Edmund Bertram, who is the only member of the family who appreciates Fanny's virtue and good sense and treats her with respect. Edmund, unfortunately, has fallen under the spell of Mary Crawford, a charming and sophisticated young woman of considerable fortune, but of shallow character and dubious morality. Even more alarming, Fanny herself is courted (ardently but whimsically) by Henry Crawford, Mary's amoral brother. Fanny rejects his proposal, drawing the rancor of the Bertram family, because she has observed Henry's inappropriate attentions to both the Bertram daughters, especially to Maria, who is already married to a wealthy but unprepossessing country squire. Eventually Fanny is vindicated when Henry seduces Maria and ruins her marriage, only to abandon her to the shame of her family and the ruin of her own position in society. Edmund is finally disillusioned both by Mary's flippant exoneration of her brother's offenses and her disdain for Edmund's vocation as a clergyman, and he marries his cousin Fanny.

The parallels to be found in *Metropolitan* are understated but unmistakable: Audrey Rouget is a shy bookish girl for whom Tom Townsend feels affection and respect, but who is overshadowed by his infatuation with the glamorous but superficial Serena Slocum. Audrey becomes, at least briefly, the sexual quarry of the sinister Rick von Sloneker, who, we have reason to believe, has "ruined" several girls, much as Henry Crawford ruins Maria in *Mansfield Park*. Just as Fanny is pressured by the Bertram family to accept Crawford's proposal, so Audrey is pushed toward von Sloneker by her friends' disapproval of the socially awkward outsider, Tom Townsend, and by his preoccupation with Serena. Audrey has too much good sense and self-respect to be deceived by a cad like Rick, just as Fanny resists the dubious Mr. Crawford; and Tom, like Edmund, is eventually disenchanted by the selfishness and insincerity of the girl who has mesmerized him sexually and realizes that he cares more for Audrey's intelligence and virtue.

More important, however, than the analogous relationships among the main characters is the overall similarity of their situations, which heightens the theme of young adults abandoned to their own injudicious devices. In *Mansfield Park*, the Bertram paterfamilias, Sir Thomas Bertram, has to make a lengthy journey to Antigua to attend to crucial business interests. While he is gone, the house is under the nominal control of his indolent wife and his snobbish, self-centered sister-in-law, who has taught his daughters to be vain and self-indulgent. The mother lacks the energy and concern, the aunt the judgment, to guide the youth of the family in prudent courses. The result is a scheme to put on an inappropriate play that will involve the young men and women in excessively familiar dialogue and scenes. Only Fanny resists, because she is sure that Sir Thomas would not approve, and she is condemned not only by the other young persons, but also by her aunt, Mrs. Norris. Tom Townsend's incredulous contempt at the notion that there is "something immoral in a group of young people putting on a play" is ironic, because the improper intimacy between Henry Crawford and Maria Bertram Rushworth occasioned by the rehearsal of their parts in the play, *Lovers' Vows*, ultimately leads to Maria's adultery and disgrace with Crawford. By the same token, the imprudent activities of the Sally Fowler Rat Pack, when they are left on their own in their parents' Manhattan apartments, give rise to cruel and degenerate behavior. At one point they engage in a tawdry game of strip poker, and even more devastating is the game of "Truth," in which the losing players are compelled to reveal their most intimate secrets. Sally uses the game to force Audrey to hear Tom Townsend confess his crush on Serena Slocum, and the game provides Cynthia McLean with the opportunity to expose her fornication with Nick Smith.

Both the play in *Mansfield Park* and the games in *Metropolitan* furnish occasions of improper familiarity and moral and physical exhibitionism with serious consequences. Like Fanny, Audrey opposes the activities that her reckless friends propose; and, if she is weaker than Fanny and finally yields to peer pressure to participate in the game of "Truth," she is also more articulate than Fanny. Her explanation of what is wrong with "Truth" is an equally good explanation of what is wrong with the amateur theatricals in the Bertram household: "There are good reasons why people don't go around telling each other their most intimate thoughts.... That's how it became a convention—people saw the harm excessive candor could do. That's why there are conventions, so people don't have to go around repeating the same mistakes over and over again." It is the responsibility of mature adults to maintain convention and with it the civilization convention protects. In *Mansfield Park* Lady Bertram and her sister Mrs. Norris fail to do this when Sir Thomas is away on an extended journey. In *Metropolitan* an entire generation has been abandoned by parents who give them free rein in empty apartments, thus leaving them in a moral wasteland without the steadying influence of inviolable tradition.

Nick Smith attempts to fill this vacuum by serving as the spokesman for traditional civilities. Although his failure is not inevitable, it is predictable, because he is not himself sufficiently mature or wise to maintain and manifest the traditional wisdom that he expounds. Nick frequently displays genuine insight and sensitivity beneath apparent flippancy. When he urges Tom not to abandon the debutante parties, he makes his case on the basis of sound, conservative moral thought. First, he undermines the reverse snobbery and self-righteousness of Tom's "Fourierist" objection "on principle" to debutante balls, which Tom admits is "the principle that one shouldn't be out eating hors d'oeuvres when you could be home worrying about the less fortunate." Nick points out that Tom himself could be considered "the less fortunate," and that he would not wish to be the object of such abstract compassion:

> I mean there's something a tiny bit arrogant about people going around feeling sorry for other people they consider "less fortunate." Are the "more fortunate" really so terrific? Do you want some much richer guy going around saying, "Poor Tom Townsend—doesn't even have a winter coat—I can't go to any more parties."

Having suggested that Tom cannot do anything in his own straitened circumstances to alleviate the poverty of those he considers "less fortunate," Nick then points out that he can be of use to the "more fortunate" girls who "are now counting on you as an escort." In making this plea, he reveals a degree of empathy for young women that is remarkable in such a young man:

> I'm not sure if you realize it, but they're at a very vulnerable point in their lives. All this is much more emotional and difficult for them than it is for us. They're on display. They've got to call guys up to invite them as escorts. And preppy girls mature socially much later than others do; for many of them this is the first serious social life they've had. If you just disappear now, they're going to take that as a personal rejection.

Naturally, this is all said with a jocular air, and Tom tries to brush it off; but Nick insists, "I'm not entirely joking," and cajoles the other boy into continuing to serve as an escort.

Yet in spite of his perspicacity, Nick cannot fulfill Sir Thomas Bertram's role of judicious patriarch. His instincts about Rick von Sloneker and Cynthia McLean are essentially accurate: they are both despicably vulgar and selfish. But Nick's own passions are not sufficiently under control for him to judge with convincing candor and disinterest. When Cynthia takes advantage of the game of "Truth" to disclose that she has slept with Nick, the others in the Rat Pack are both dismayed and somewhat pleased to discover the flaws in Nick's self-assured manner of moral and social superiority. "After all that about what a terrible slut she was," a disgusted and probably jealous Jane cries out; and Nick can only answer weakly, "But a very attractive slut." Charlie complains, "So you're just another hypocrite," to which Nick answers, with more vigor, "That's not hypocrisy. It's sin." Cynthia sneers at the notion of sin, and it is a measure of Nick's traditional orientation that he rejects the typically modern view that hypocrisy is the only sin, that nothing is evil in itself. Calling Cynthia "a very attractive slut" is an indirect, oxymoronic way of confessing that desire is not self-validating, that fallen human beings can be tempted by what they know to be evil—

can lust after what is, to the higher self, repulsive. Charlie, however, in a larger sense than he realizes, is correct in calling Nick a
"hypocrite": he is a hypocrite in the root meaning of the word,
"actor." Nick is playing a role that is beyond his capacity.

This is very evident in his attacks on Rick von Sloneker and in
their eventual confrontation. Nick rightly perceives that Rick has a
crude, exploitative attitude toward women, and there are, doubtless, rumors in circulation about his abusive sexual adventures.
When he admits to Tom that there never was a "Polly Perkins," a
girl who supposedly committed suicide after Rick seduced her and
coerced her into "pulling a train" for a group of his friends, it becomes clear that Nick has no firsthand knowledge of Baron von
Sloneker's misdeeds, whatever they may be. To be sure, Cynthia
has sufficient doubts about Rick's innocence to admit that she has
heard of the nonexistent Polly and to accuse her of being a "patho-
logical liar," but our qualms about Nick's accusations are still not
much alleviated by his explanation to Tom that "'Polly Perkins' is
essentially a composite, based on real people, like *New York Magazine* does." Despite a measure of vindication, Nick fares even worse
in his face-to-face confrontation with von Sloneker. Having been
forced to admit that he made up the composite victim, Nick brings
up Cathy Livingstone, presumably a name attached to one of the
rumors, and it turns out that the "Polly Perkins" story was very near
the truth. Von Sloneker's explanation is more of a lame concession:
"Anything which went on between Cathy Livingstone and me was
entirely personal, entirely private, and has nothing to do with her
suicide, which was months afterwards." Nevertheless, when Rick
bloodies Nick's nose with an unexpected punch, the latter is effectively silenced and gets no sympathy from the Rat Pack. Jane sums
up the general attitude:

> Why should we believe you over Rick? We know you're a hypocrite.
> We know your "Polly Perkins" story was a fabrication,...that you're
> completely impossible and out of control with some sort of drug prob-
> lem and a fixation on what you consider Rick von Sloneker's wicked-
> ness. You're a snob, a sexist, totally obnoxious and tiresome. And lately
> you've gotten just weird. Why should we believe anything you say?

Only Tom remains loyal to the boy who befriended him in the street
and introduced him to the group, and it is on Tom that Nick's influence is both profound and beneficial.

As an outsider to whom Nick Smith is a new friend, Tom is able
to the make the most of Nick's genuine insight in a way that seems
impossible for the others, who have known him and his weaknesses for years and who have wearied of him. Nick's appreciation
for the importance of traditional virtues becomes most explicit in a
scene where he is extolling the merits of detachable collars. He
typically introduces an important idea under the guise of a trivial
preoccupation. Wearing a detachable collar, Nick maintains, is "a
small thing, but symbolically important." "Our parents' generation,"
he continues, "was never interested in keeping up standards. They
wanted to [be] 'happy,' but of course the last way to be 'happy' is to
make it your objective in life." For a youth still in adolescence, this
is an extraordinarily shrewd moral claim, which he certainly did
not learn from the father who has abandoned his mother for another (probably younger) woman. Indeed, both the youthful characters in the film and their generally AWOL parents lead blighted
lives because they have no objective beyond an always elusive
sense of immediate well-being. When Tom then wonders whether
their own generation is better than their parents', Nick replies in a
fashion that is puzzling, impassioned, and profound:

> It's far worse. Our generation is probably the worst since...the Protes-
> tant Reformation. It's barbaric, but a barbarism even worse than the
> old-fashioned kind. Now barbarism is cloaked with all sorts of self-
> righteousness and moral superiority....

As Nick trails off Tom rightly observes that he is "talking about a lot more than detachable collars."

The full significance of the condemnation of self-righteous barbarism only comes later in the film: when Jane and Cynthia proclaim the virtues of candor and openness for a game deceitfully called "Truth" as a pretext for exposing and humiliating others and manipulating their feelings; when Nick's confessed fornication is condemned only as hypocrisy and the very idea of sin is scorned; and when most of the group dismisses Nick's accusations against Rick von Sloneker, although the latter is obviously guilty in some fashion. The reference to the Protestant Reformation is pertinent insofar as it represents an overturning of a communal tradition of worship in the interest of the individual's apprehension of personal righteousness imputed through his unique relationship with God. It is of course not necessary that Nick be altogether aware of these details for the reference to work. Its relevance is underscored when, as Nick retreats "upstate" to face "a stepmother of untrammeled malevolence—very possibly to be killed," we see him for the last time in the film walking away in Grand Central Station to the sounds of Luther's hymn, "A Mighty Fortress Is Our God."

Tom's modest comic heroism, which draws inspiration from Nick Smith, is underscored by his equivocal relationship with Charlie Black. Charlie is the originator of the acronym U.H.B., for "urban haute bourgeoisie," which he wishes to substitute for terms like "preppy" and "WASP." His melancholy obsession with what he assumes will be the inevitable downward mobility of this privileged class, as they are displaced by youths who are more aggressive and competent because they are comparatively less affluent, is doubtless the source of the film's lugubrious subtitle, *Doomed Bourgeois in Love*. A rather feckless character, Charlie berates Nick through much of the film for having befriended Tom, whom he regards as a cad who has abused Audrey's affection. The real source of Charlie's animosity, as Nick points out, is jealousy—Tom having won the heart of the girl for whom Charlie has silently longed. Yet the tale concludes with Tom and Charlie as allies in the "rescue" of Audrey from the clutches of Rick von Sloneker in his sinister beach house in Southampton, and it is Tom who overcomes the hesitation of his new comrade and insists that they must take action. The kernel of Charlie's ineffectuality emerges in a chance conversation in a bar with one Dick Edwards, a middle-aged "uhb," who laments his own failure and envies success in a way that at first seems to corroborate Charlie's fatalistic pessimism about his class. Edwards, however, denies the determinism:

> You're partly right: Some of the successful contemporaries I mentioned were not from an "uhb" background. But some were. You'll have to accept it—not everyone from our background is doomed to failure.

Charlie's refusal to accept responsibility for his own destiny is a mark of his personal insufficiency.

The contrast with Tom is striking, and in some measure his independence and his sense that he has some control over his future are a result of Nick's influence. At one point when he is trying to overcome Charlie's reluctance to seek out Audrey at von Sloneker's place in Southampton, Tom says, "If only Nick were here—he'd know how to handle this." This is not, however, an admission of defeat, but Tom's assertion that he must act as he thinks his absent friend would under the same circumstances. A second and even more important influence on Tom is Audrey herself, not only because of his growing romantic attraction to her, but also because, like Nick, she sets a standard to which he must aspire. Explaining to an incredulous Jane how his "big night" with Serena Slocum has only made him value Audrey, he suggests that her attraction is precisely her capacity to draw him out of himself into an undiscovered intellectual and moral realm: "There's something really great about being with Audrey—I mean, I think I prefer arguing with Audrey to agreeing with Serena or someone else." And Tom is undeterred by Jane's revelation that Audrey (partly through Jane's intervention) regards him as "a total jerk" and "despises" him. In the event, Tom's confrontation with Rick is more successful than Nick's. Rick surprises Tom with a punch as he had Nick and threatens further violence with help of Lemley, but Tom keeps his wits about him and brandishes the toy derringer that he has rescued from the trash outside his father's apartment, securing his escape along with Audrey and Charlie.

The toy derringer is a symbol of what Tom has in common with his improbable mentor, Nick; both have been in effect abandoned by their fathers. When they come upon the toys stacked up for trash pickup outside the apartment building of Tom's father, Nick remarks, "The childhood of our whole generation is represented here, and they're just throwing it out." To a certain extent, the remark applies to the generation itself, as well as its toys. When Nick leaves New York to visit his father and stepmother, he makes Tom promise to investigate should he die in their company. This hyperbole is typical of Nick's often hysterical manner, but it reflects a genuine anxiety on his part about his status with his father, and hence his position in the world. Tom's shabby treatment at the hands of his father is even more devastating. Having discovered that his father has moved out of the city and deprived him of an anticipated trust fund, Tom sums up his situation with a doleful understatement in sharp contrast to Nick's exaggeration: "He moves to another state without telling me, doesn't call or write for months, and basically has me disinherited. Obviously our relationship was not what I thought it was." It is Nick who defines the abandonment of his generation in a poignantly bitter statement: "The most important thing to realize about parents is that there's absolutely nothing you can do about them."

In conclusion, two points remain to be made. First, for all the seriousness of the situation dramatized in *Metropolitan*, and despite the real triumph attained by Tom and Audrey at the close, this is a thoroughly comic film that undermines the pretensions of all its characters. Nick's attempt to serve as the voice of wisdom is compromised by his pomposity and his personal failings, and his departure is inglorious. Tom's victorious rescue of Audrey, her chastity intact, is treated with gentle irony, in part by the ridiculous figure that Rick von Sloneker cuts as a villain and in part by the adolescent foibles of the hero and heroine. Even Audrey, who is finally the most engaging as well as the most moral character in the film, is wracked by childish insecurity. When von Sloneker, apparently disappointed by Audrey's resistance to his seductive charms, calls her a "flat-chested, goody-goody pain-in-the-neck," Tom's rejoinder is that she is not a "goody-goody." In the final scene, when they are safely out of von Sloneker's lair, Audrey asks Tom, with evident concern, "Do you really think I'm flat-chested?" If the triumph is somewhat diminished by such reminders of the principal characters' immaturity, it suffers further when we realize that their situation has not changed at the film's end. They are still abandoned by their parents' generation, not only having to solve their own problems without adult guidance, but having to make up their own rules for living. The final scene shows Tom, Audrey, and Charlie trying to hitchhike back to New York, and no one is stopping. This is Whit Stillman's final image of the youthful "uhbs," the abandoned generation of *Metropolitan*—a long way from home on an empty road, not really sure how to get to where they belong.

Five

In Defense of Virtue:
Whit Stillman's *Metropolitan*

Joseph Alulis

METROPOLITAN BELONGS TO a popular movie genre: it is a "coming of age" film. What distinguishes it from most films of this sort is the earnest class-consciousness of its characters. There is a hint of Karl Marx in the film's subtitle, *Doomed Bourgeois In Love*. But the title itself suggests the film's concern with social class: the metropolis or "mother city" is a rich city. A city (*civitas*) is constituted in the decisive sense not of buildings and streets but of citizens (*cives*). And the citizens who are properly of, or belonging to, the rich city are the wealthy. The group of eight young people whose story the film tells, the "Sally Fowler Rat Pack" or "SFRP," belong, by and large, to this class. Moreover, these young people, or some of them at least, are very self-conscious about their class status. Charlie Black, the group's "intellectual," is concerned with the appropriate name for his class:

> I don't think "preppy" is a very useful term. It might be descriptive for someone still in school or college, but it's ridiculous to have to refer to a man in his seventies—like Averell Harriman—as a "preppy." And none of the other terms people use—WASP, PLU, et cetera—are much use,

either.... That's why I prefer to use the term "U.H.B."...an acronym for "urban haute bourgeoisie."

In the scene immediately preceding this one Audrey Rouget, the heroine of the film, implicitly compares the group to the members of an aristocracy when she comments that their social life makes her think of *War and Peace*. Nick Smith, as self-reflective as Charlie but ironic rather than ardent in this thought, completes Audrey's comparison by distinguishing between a titled and an untitled aristocracy. Their group belongs to the latter kind.

But if their class is untitled, the "class prerogatives" it possesses are based entirely on private means; they are not "publicly acknowledged and secure." Society will not hold them up; as Charlie notes, there are no barriers to their "downward social mobility." Charlie goes further and asserts that "the whole preppy class" is "doomed" to a "downward fall." But this idea of class decline is a kind of avoidance on his part. "That would be too easy," an older person of his class tells him. "You'll have to accept it—not everyone from our background is doomed to failure." It is a question of personal responsibility.

In this way *Metropolitan* is a true "coming of age" film: it deals with the anxiety of growing up, the fear of personal failure—not just in one's work, as productive and creative beings—but in life as a whole, as sexual and thinking beings as well. It depicts eight young people dealing with this anxiety more or less thoughtfully and shows them meeting the challenge of growing up both more and less successfully. In doing so it not only attempts to answer the questions, "What does success mean?" and "What does it take to succeed?" It gives those answers a political dimension.

Success, *Metropolitan* suggests, depends upon the traditional intellectual and moral virtues—preeminently, practical wisdom and temperance. In particular, the film portrays practical wisdom, in the most bourgeois of lights, as respect for convention. The story consists largely of the education of the film's hero, Tom Townsend, in the importance of respect for convention. That education is provided, most importantly, by the film's heroine, Audrey, who because she understands the value of convention also appreciates the limits of its value. In conveying this lesson, the film serves as something of an apologia for the bourgeois regime. The just regime is the one that accords prerogative only to a class composed of persons possessed of practical wisdom and only insofar as they possess it.

The question of the meaning of personal success is raised explicitly early in the film, on the first day of the story's fortnight. Tom, on his introduction to the group, identifies himself as a Fourierist. Shortly afterward, Charlie challenges him.

> *Charlie:* Fourierism was tried in the nineteenth century and
>   failed. Wasn't Brook Farm Fourierist? It failed.
> *Tom:*   That's debatable.
> *Charlie:* That Brook Farm failed?
> *Tom:*   That it ceased to exist, I'll grant you. Whether it
>   was really a failure, I don't think can be definitively
>   said.
> *Charlie:* For me ceasing to exist is failure. That's pretty definitive.
> *Tom:*   Everyone ceases to exist. That doesn't mean
>   everyone's a failure.

The first lesson about success and failure is that death, precisely as the great equalizer, provides no standard. Excellence in life is not simply a question of the preservation of life or acquisition of the means by which life is preserved and made comfortable.

The response by the SFRP's three other thoughtful members to Charlie's warning of doom elaborates this idea. Nick's comment simply equates success with wealth. In anticipation of his failure, he says, with a meaningful look at his girlfriend, Jane Clarke, that he plans to "marry an extremely rich woman." Surprisingly, in view of his idealistic defense of Brook Farm, Tom makes the same equation. In professing indifference to the prospect of the failure of his peers he in effect treats failure as absence of wealth: "it wouldn't be any great tragedy if some of these people lost their class prerogatives." In short, success consists in the enjoyment of an abundance of the conveniences and amusements of life, that is, wealth. Later, when Tom wishes to impress Serena Slocum, an attractive young woman with "an incredible number of boyfriends," he chooses a restaurant strictly on the basis of how expensive it is.

Crassness and vulgarity respectively taint Nick and Tom's responses. Neither speaker may be relied upon to have a sound idea of what constitutes success or failure. Audrey's response, however, reflecting as it does her virtuous character, gives better guidance. To Tom's dismissive comment that it would be no "tragedy" if the whole preppy class should fail, she replies: "it's not a question of losing 'class prerogatives,' whatever that means, but the prospect of wasting your whole productive life, of personal failure." Failure for Audrey is waste, the improper use of faculties and powers. By the same token, success is a productive—proper or creative, and therefore satisfying—employment of one's talents and capacities. Judgment of success or failure on these terms is independent of questions of wealth. We are what we do, not what income we have. Dick Edwards, the older man with whom Charlie and Tom talk about success and failure, echoes this idea. "The acid test is if you get any pleasure from answering the question, 'What do you do?' I can't bear it."

A second measure of success has to do with personal relations and has two dimensions, happiness and duty. Continuing her reflection on Charlie's speech about failure, Audrey remarks to Tom, "I think my father considers himself a failure, although I don't think he's one. Probably few people's lives match their own expectations." What we see of Audrey's parents' residence makes it clear that her family is affluent. If her father thinks himself a failure, it is not because he is not making money. Perhaps it is because, like Dick Edwards, he can't bear his work. Audrey's positive view of him, on the other hand, reflects her personal experience of her father, namely, his care for her and for their family, care that, in part, involves material support. His wealth provides the equipment for his success, but the success she sees in his life consists primarily in how he uses that wealth in fulfillment of his duties. In the film's first scene we see Audrey's caring mother, but we never see her father. We see a stable and loving home for the children, Audrey and her younger brother, but not parents who are happy in their lives together. Perhaps this is the expectation that his life failed to match?

However it may be with Audrey's father, something like this is suggested about Nick's father, who, in some respects, is the opposite of Audrey's. Nick's parents are divorced. So far from seeing his father as caring for him, Nick fears for his life when he is called to visit his father and stepmother. Nick makes no comment on whether he sees his father as a success or a failure. He does, however, suggest that he is neither happy nor dutiful. "Our parents' generation was never interested in keeping up standards. They wanted to be 'happy,' but of course the last way to be 'happy' is to make it your objective in life." Nick's father, one infers, put happiness before "standards" in leaving Nick and his mother and yet has failed to attain his objective. The thought emerges that one may be dutiful without being happy (Audrey's father) but that one cannot be happy if one is not dutiful (Nick's father). The best course is to make duty, or keeping up standards, the principal objective and hope that this may be combined with happiness, convinced that there can be no happiness in a life that departs from standards. In the course of the

story, Nick repeats his father's mistake in a lesser key, by his un-
faithfulness to Jane.

In relations with others, then, success is measured in two ways.
One way is duty: one lives one's life in conformity to the group's
standards. The second way is happiness. In what happiness consists is suggested by the story of Tom, Serena, and Audrey.

For the greater part of the film, Tom thinks he is in love with
Serena Slocum. On the first night we learn of his letters to Serena
and that they have apparently broken up. Three nights later, however, the relationship is revived, and six nights after that Tom publicly confesses to the group, "I've had a crush on Serena, with some
ups and downs, for over two years. Recently it seems to have developed into something more serious." In between the fourth and
tenth nights we see Tom treating Serena's letters to him like pre-
cious documents and setting up her picture by his bedside.

During all this time we also see Audrey in love with Tom. On
the first night on which the two meet, we learn that Serena read
Tom's letters aloud and Audrey thinks they were quite good. Later
it is Audrey that elicits from Tom his declaration that he and Serena
have broken up. That same evening, between the former and the
latter conversations, we see a brief scene of intense discussion between Audrey and Sally that consists entirely in the following exchange, accompanied by much girlish laughter:

> *Sally:*   You really feel that way?
> *Audrey:* I really do.
> *Sally:*   Really?
> *Audrey:* Really.

The viewer is left to surmise what might be the subject of this
dialogue; subsequent developments lead one to think that Audrey
has just confessed to her friend her attraction to Tom. When Tom
accompanies Audrey home the next night, she gives him an inno-

cent peck of a kiss. The following night, when Tom abandons Audrey at a social event in order to accompany Serena home, where
she gives him a kiss that is not at all innocent, Audrey is clearly
crushed. Nonetheless, she refuses to give up her pursuit of Tom. To
her friend Jane's advice the next day that she not get involved with
him, Audrey replies, "Tom is the only guy I've ever really liked in
my whole life." That this is not mere infatuation Audrey makes clear.
When Jane protests that Audrey hardly knows Tom, the following
exchange takes place.

> *Audrey:* I know him very well.
> *Jane:*   You couldn't—you only just met.
> *Audrey:* Well, I do.

As it turns out, Audrey has gotten to know Tom through his
letters to Serena that she begged of Serena when the latter was
about to throw them away. During all these successive evenings
we see Tom and Audrey engaged in lively conversation about books
and authors, ideas and experiences. Finally, Tom's public profes-
sion that his attachment to Serena is "serious" puts an end, at least
temporarily, to Audrey's pursuit.

In the event, it is Audrey, not Serena, whom Tom really loves.
He discovers this on the occasion of his expensive date with Serena when he learns the fate of his letters: they were of no value to
Serena but meant a great deal to Audrey. It is Audrey, not Serena,
who shares Tom's idea of what is important in life and for whom he
cares. As he later tells Jane:

> On the big night I'd looked forward to for a week, I started feeling this
> incredible loneliness being with Serena and nostalgia for all those con-
> versations with Audrey before the big blow-up, and this was before I
> knew anything about the letters. I mean, I think I prefer arguing with
> Audrey to agreeing with Serena or someone else. In fact, I had only had
> that calmly unemotional perspective on my relationship with Serena

for a little while when I started feeling this warm glow at the prospect
of seeing Audrey here again tonight.

The happiness one experiences in love is the "warm glow" the
lover feels at the prospect of being in the company of the beloved,
it is the absence of "loneliness" in the company of the beloved, it is
the pleasure one takes in conversation with the beloved. Success
in one's personal relations involves the experience of such happiness, but only in the context of a life lived according to the dictates
of duty.

That *Metropolitan* teaches this lesson—that happiness consists
in such pleasure and is greatly to be desired, but that duty or ad-
herence to standards comes first—is underscored by the role Jane
Austen's *Persuasion* plays in the film. For that is precisely the theme
of this novel. In *Persuasion*, Anne Elliot, the novel's virtuous heroine, yields to the persuasion of a loving guardian, Lady Russell, to
decline the marriage proposal of the man she loves, Frederick
Wentworth. She sacrifices her happiness to the duty of filial obedi-
ence. At the end of eight years, however, Frederick Wentworth returns to Anne's social circle and this time the obstacles to marriage
present on the earlier occasion no longer prevail. In accepting a
second proposal, Anne justifies her first refusal, though it cost them
both eight years of happiness.

> I must believe I was right, much as I suffered from it, that I was per-
> fectly right in being guided by the friend...[who] to me...was in the
> place of a parent.... I was right in submitting to her, and...if I had done
> otherwise, I should have suffered more in continuing the engagement
> than I did even in giving it up, because I should have suffered in my
> conscience.

Persuasion is referred to twice in the film. Early on, Audrey
tells Tom that it is one of her favorite books. Subsequently, Tom
tells her that he is reading the book and likes it. Moreover, there is
this parallel in the two stories. In *Persuasion*, on his return after

eight years, Frederick pays court to an attractive, eligible young woman, Henrietta Musgrove, whom he thinks he loves. But Henrietta is far inferior in character to Anne and, in fact, Frederick does not really love her; he still loves Anne. The relations of Frederick, Henrietta, and Anne resemble those of Tom, Serena, and Audrey. Finally, the title of the novel reflects not only Lady Russell's initial persuasion of Anne to decline Frederick's proposal, but Anne's persuasion of Frederick to propose a second time. Anne succeeds. She wins for herself a role—wife, mistress of a household, and prospective mother—to which she is perfectly suited by talent and inclination; she wins the man she loves; and she does all in a manner that accords with the standards of her society.

In *Metropolitan*, Audrey is equally successful in a similar way: she persuades Tom that he really loves her and brings him to act publicly on that persuasion. Audrey's triumph suggests that she will escape the doom Charlie foresees for the members of his class. She possesses the qualities necessary for success. But we must now consider in more detail what precisely these qualities are.

*M*etropolitan ends with the three friends, Audrey, Charlie, and Tom, on the road together, "in the desolate Southampton of late December," as Stillman's stage directions put it, making their way home to Manhattan. They have a long way to go and the journey promises to be arduous, but the viewer is inclined to be hopeful. Their situation is a metaphor for their position in life: they are only at the start of their adult lives and many perils lie before them, but one is entitled to be sanguine about their prospects because of what one has seen of them. Earlier in the film we saw Nick depart by train—significantly, on track 21—on a journey fraught with danger. Nick's departure is made, appropriately, in grand style, and in contrast to the more modest scene at the film's end. But Nick is making his trip alone (the stage direction describes his wave good-bye as "poignant") while Audrey, Tom, and Charlie, going together, have each other for support. Of the eight young people in the Sally Fowler Rat Pack, it is these three who have the greatest chance for success. The qualities necessary for success are the qualities they display and, in the case of Charlie and Tom, acquire in the course of the story. The qualities that are singled out are practical wisdom and temperance.

The two virtues are closely related: traditionally temperance is seen as preserving practical wisdom. If practical wisdom, or prudence, is more important as pointing out the way, temperance is necessary lest one lose one's guide. Nick's failure to resist Cynthia's seduction despite his appreciation of the importance of standards underscores the importance of this virtue.

The characters in the film can be ranked in attractiveness roughly according to their possession of this virtue. Of the SFRP, surely Fred, who drinks too much, and Cynthia, who offends against chastity (and is fairly shameless about it), are the least attractive and Audrey the most, with the others distributed between these two poles. The fact that Jane does not rank as highly as Audrey points up the distinction between chastity and coldness. Jane's reaction to Nick's fall seems less an instance of rectitude than a failure of charity and judgment. The villain of the film, Rick von Sloneker, takes pride in his sexual excesses and the film ends with Tom and Charlie's rescue of Audrey from von Sloneker's hands. In fact, however, Audrey's chastity protects her. The image of Audrey, serene in her virtue within von Sloneker's seedy lair, utterly impervious to his seduction, the more for seeing him as ridiculous, marks the film's comic tableau of the triumph of good over evil. *Metropolitan* appears in the end as among other things a very witty defense of chastity.

The film gives greater attention to the meaning and importance of the intellectual virtue of practical wisdom. Four of the eight members of the SFRP are distinguished by their intellect—Audrey, Char-

lie, Nick, and Tom. Of these, Charlie with his defense of the bourgeoisie and Tom with his allusions to Veblen and Fourier attend
more to society at large. Audrey and Nick are more concerned with
individuals. While Charlie and Tom speak of the fate of classes,
Audrey focuses on the person: "'These people' are everyone I know."
Nick mocks Charlie's concern with accurately naming their class
but shows sensitivity to the needs of the members of that class who
are part of his circle. Charlie's seriousness makes him seem most
like an intellectual while Nick's irony makes him seem the least.
His response to Charlie's prophecy of doom for their class, that he
plans to marry money, seems less crass when read in light of his
irony. In general, Nick is very thoughtful, as suggested by his reflections about happiness and standards. He begins that speech
with a recommendation of detachable collars. When he has fin-
ished Tom comments, "You're obviously talking about a lot more
than detachable collars...." to which Nick replies, "Yeah, I am."
This exchange serves as the key to most of Nick's remarks. Though
Nick fails to act wisely, he plays a large role in Tom's education.
Principally, however, the film's exploration of the meaning of practical wisdom centers on the three figures with whom the film ends,
Audrey, Tom, and Charlie.

Metropolitan highlights two particular aspects of practical wisdom: respect for convention and initiative. Audrey possesses both
these qualities while, at the start of the film, Tom and Charlie are
each deficient in one. Tom appears as the vehement critic of conventional society. His failure to appreciate the value of convention
is a defect. Nonetheless, this failing is related to a strength. His
reformist zeal bespeaks a willingness to take bold action when this
seems called for. Thus, the plan to rescue Audrey is, from start to
finish, all Tom's initiative. At least in part, it is this positive aspect of
his unconventionality that attracts Audrey: "One thing I like about
him is that he doesn't say all the expected things."

Charlie, on the other hand, is too much the theorist or spectator. He is critical of Tom because he is jealous of him, and he is
jealous because he is attracted to Audrey. But as Nick points out, he
fails to act on his attraction and contents himself with vain criticism
of his rival. Still, Charlie does understand the value of convention.
Nick comments at one point that "Charlie's standard of polite behavior is...exaggerated." Next to Audrey, Charlie is the staunchest
advocate of good conduct. Audrey and Charlie are the only members of the SFRP who don't take part in the group's strip poker game.

Part of the action of the film is intended to show how Tom and
Charlie acquire the part of practical wisdom each lacks at the start.
Thus, in a scene faintly resembling Pierre Bezukhor's declaration
of love to Natasha Rostov in *War and Peace,* Charlie does finally
come to declare himself to Audrey.[3] Though his declaration is not
welcomed at the moment it is made, he is rewarded the next day by
a warm response from Audrey. Finally, in the penultimate scene of
the film, there is between the two, registered for the viewer only in
Charlie's wry expression, a significant meeting of the eyes.

The more striking change is in Tom. The attachments he forms,
especially to Nick, Charlie, and Audrey, reflect his transformation.
Early on Nick challenges Tom's opposition to his class's conventions as a kind of arrogance. Subsequently Nick serves as Tom's
mentor in the practices and rules of his class until, in the end, Tom
becomes himself a defender of these conventions. Thus it is Tom
who questions von Sloneker's scorn of convention as a defect of
character: the failure to treat convention seriously does not prove
that one is serious but proves rather the opposite. Nick's gift to Tom
of his top hat when the two part at Grand Central Station is a nice
expression of the change their association has worked in Tom.

If Nick guides Tom largely with friendly advice, Charlie stirs his
conscience. When he abandons Audrey at the dance at the St. Regis,
Charlie's reproach, that his carelessness about social form is a kind

of egoism, makes a strong impression on him. Tom's gentle tribute to Charlie at the end, when the two have joined forces to rescue Audrey—"you're not such a bad fellow"—reflects the new respect he has acquired for the moral significance of good social form. Tom's last words in the film, moreover, responding to Audrey's question about whether she is flat-chested—"you don't want to overdo it"— shows the appreciation for the importance of tact in social relations that he has learned from Nick and Charlie.

Finally, and more generally, Tom's growing appreciation of Audrey—her taste in literature, her conversation and society, her judgment in matters of personal relations—is a measure of his growing understanding of the value of convention. Part of what is attractive about Audrey is her graceful courtesy, a quality that colors and enriches all her other attractions.

The strongest lesson Tom gets in the importance of convention, however, comes not from the members of the SFRP but from his father. During the course of the film Tom learns that his father has discarded Tom's childhood possessions that were in his care, has moved away without informing Tom, and has revoked a trust fund established for Tom's benefit. In this case, Tom bears the brunt of someone else's egoism. His father's contempt for convention, from the simplest forms of courtesy to the bestowal of property by one generation upon the next, enable Tom to see clearly the contribution to a decent social life that convention makes.

While Tom and Charlie need to acquire these different parts of practical wisdom, Audrey possesses them from the start. She more clearly displays and articulates the value of each quality. And nowhere is Audrey's prudence more evident than in her objection to the game of "Truth" on the grounds of respect for convention. This episode marks a turning point in the relations of all the characters. After this evening they are all together only once more and then in a very tense and strained atmosphere.

The game involves a kind of lottery in which the person desig-
nated must "answer with absolute honesty whatever question [he]
is asked, no matter how embarrassing," and indeed, "the more embarrassing the better." Audrey objects that "telling each other their
most intimate thoughts" could be dangerous. When Sally, who has
proposed the game, replies that she doesn't "see what's dangerous
about it," Audrey gives a succinct account of the origin and value of
convention. "You don't have to. Other people have. That's how it
became a convention—people saw the harm excessive candor could
do." Social convention reflects the prudence of past generations,
gained by centuries of experience. It is a super-foresight that by
supplementing the small portion each individual possesses ren-
ders him wiser in his conduct than he would otherwise be. Without meeting this argument, Cynthia makes the very fact that the rule
is external to the individual a matter of objection: "You admit that
it's basically *just* a social convention, then." When Audrey persists
in her objection, Cynthia makes an utterly deceitful argument in
the guise of an appeal to reason. "Let's discuss this. Basically, what
this game requires is complete candor—which means openness,
honesty. I don't see how that can be bad." In the event, not only is
harm done but it is clear this harm is exactly what Cynthia intended. When it comes to her turn to be questioned, Cynthia has,
as she expects, an opportunity to reveal her sexual encounter with
Nick, thereby injuring his reputation in the group and ruining his
relationship with Jane. Her motive for this is the desire to be re-
venged on Nick because he has been critical of her. What makes
her revenge more sweet is that Nick's criticism has been precisely
of her loose sexual behavior.

When it is Tom's turn to be questioned, Jane asks him about
his romantic interests, confident he will confess his attachment to
Serena. While Jane in effect encourages Tom to at least name Audrey in second place, something that his honesty apparently pro-

hibits, she must have foreseen that however Tom answered, his candor would hurt Audrey. Jane nonetheless asks the question to vindicate her own opinion that Audrey made a mistake to get involved with Tom. Given her assertion that honesty can do no harm, it is ironic to see Cynthia, out of consideration for Audrey, attempt to steer Tom to an answer that will soften the blow to her friend. In short, the game is not about honesty or truth but egoism. Convention emerges as a social form that checks our selfish passions in our relations with each other.

There is another reason to object to this game which the story makes clear, namely, that in many cases we cannot report or reveal the truth about ourselves because we do not know it. Thus, Tom's declaration that he loves Serena, not Audrey, and that if this relationship fails, he will not consider another any time soon, turns out to be wrong. Convention creates for the truth a space shielded from our ignorance of our own motives and desires. It acknowledges that the truth is veiled and attempts to forestall the deception attendant on vain pretenses of lifting the veil.

The film suggests that this lesson about truth applies not just to matters of personal relations and self-knowledge, but to our knowledge of ultimate things as well. From the very beginning, we see that at least the more thoughtful members of the SFRP are concerned with questions about ultimate things. On the first night of the story we see Charlie in earnest conversation with Cynthia about the existence of God. Insofar as we are thinking beings, success in growing up involves some kind of resolution of these questions. *Metropolitan* suggests that religious ritual serves the same function in ultimate matters as convention does in social matters. Thus, when Nick speaks of the "barbarism" of the "Protestant Reformation," he is referring to the Reformers' attempt to tear aside the veil. But no more than with happiness is the truth obtained when it is made the direct object of our endeavor. Rather, such an attempt leaves one with Cynthia's complete absence of thought. On Christmas Eve we are given two images of possible responses to ultimate questions. At the Townsend household we see Tom alone with the television on in the background, with a burning yule log on the screen and a tinny, elevator music version of "Jingle Bells" playing. In immediate juxtaposition to this, we see Audrey at midnight mass at St. Thomas Episcopal Church. The church's architecture is Gothic and on a scale sufficient to make it an appropriate seat for a bishop; the pews are full of people, a magnificent procession makes its way around the building, and the assembled community is singing "O Come All Ye Faithful." The stage direction in the shooting script reads "Majestic ceremony. Beautiful Christmas music."

Audrey's sure grasp of the way respect for convention is a part of practical wisdom suggests an understanding that bespeaks a capacity for personal success. But simply being conventional is hardly a formula for success in life. To this must be added the resourcefulness and capacity for action that I have called initiative. Such initiative might well involve departing from the dictate of convention on occasion. It is this kind of initiative Audrey shows in going with Cynthia to von Sloneker's Southampton residence.

As Charlie and Tom both observe separately, this is not something Jane Austen would have approved. It is very unconventional. Yet the action has this beneficial result: it draws the three friends closer together by giving them an opportunity to express in deed their respect and regard for each other. In particular, by her unconventional venture, Audrey elicits from Tom a public acknowledgment that he cares for her. Does the film justify seeing the result as Audrey's intention? Why exactly does she go to von Sloneker's with Cynthia?

Certainly, as the "Truth" game suggests, the two young women are at opposite poles in character. Insofar as von Sloneker is Cynthia's type, his company will not be at all attractive to Audrey. But it is precisely the great difference between Audrey and Cynthia that, for two reasons, explains her action. First, Audrey tells Tom that Cynthia was especially insistent that Audrey go with her. One surmises Cynthia wanted the cover of Audrey's respectability for her action. As her reaction to the appearance of Tom and Charlie suggests, she is not entirely shameless. Second, and more important, is Audrey's curiosity about Cynthia's character. The day after the "Truth" game, in conversation with Jane, Audrey seems to question her own judgment. "Maybe Cynthia's right." Jane is unwilling to even consider the possibility but Audrey persists: "Her essential view is that experience is good, and she's set out to acquire it. I've been just the opposite. Everything's been in my imagination—all the romance imaginary, nothing real."

One explanation, then, is that she embraces an opportunity to spend time with Cynthia to test whether Cynthia's approach to life is right. She need not go so far along the way as Cynthia to get a better look at it. Audrey can rely upon her character to protect her in this venture and thus she can satisfy her questioning without imperiling her judgment.

But perhaps joined with that is the thought that her action might prompt an effort to rescue her. If it does not, she has lost nothing. But if it does, she has gained precisely what she longs for, a testament of real regard from someone for whom she cares.

The very speech she gives to Jane comparing herself and Cynthia lends support to this view. She has a rich imagination that has been occupied with romantic pictures. Insofar as *War and Peace* has fed that imagination, she must remember how Natasha is rescued from an elopement that is little better than an abduction, and how Pierre, her protector, confronts the dissolute member of their social circle who would have ruined her. The difference is that here, Audrey plays both author and heroine and, as author, writes for herself a part that reflects less poorly on her character.

The next question is whether she has any reason to think any-one would come to her rescue, in particular, Tom. Certainly she has Charlie's recent expression of affection and evidence of his wish to protect her from harm. But Charlie is not one to whom one would look for decisive action. Tom is the person to be counted upon in such a case. Now, the last time she saw Tom was the evening Nick and von Sloneker clashed. Tom's show of support for Nick that evening makes clear that he shares Nick's view of von Sloneker as a threat to respectable young women. She has reason to think Tom will learn of her whereabouts in precisely the way he does learn of it, through association with the SFRP that by this time has become habitual for him. The "claustrophobic" atmosphere of the group upon which Audrey comments is another way of saying that every-one in the group comes to know everyone else's doings. Finally, she knows Tom's character well enough to know that the closer he gets to Serena Slocum the more he will realize that his attraction to her is an illusion. The very fact that Serena had quite recently been von Sloneker's girlfriend and that Tom has come to have an entirely negative opinion of von Sloneker are enough to guarantee this. In *Persuasion,* when Anne Elliot learns Frederick Wentworth is free of any engagement to marry Henrietta Musgrove, she seeks out and fully exploits any occasion that brings herself and Frederick to-gether, so that she might persuade him to a second proposal. So Audrey contrives a situation which might bring Tom to realize how much he cares for her and to act upon it. If this was her intent, her plan was anything but certain of success. But as a rule, great gain involves great risk. Audrey's triumph in the end is a testament to both her practical wisdom and her temperance. Her small success suggests that the same means will secure her greater success in the future.

Metropolitan gives this story of the promise of personal success and failure a political significance. In sharing their fears about the future, the young people reflect upon the social character of the privileges they enjoy. Society will not hold them up; it does not guarantee their advantages as would be the case in a titled aristocracy. In the bourgeois regime, there are no unmerited privileges and failure is punished pretty quickly. As Charlie warns his peers, "the downward fall is going to be very fast." By the same token, merit is quickly rewarded. The other face of social mobility in America is "the comparative ease of moving upward." This assessment conforms to the picture Alexis de Tocqueville drew of American society in an earlier age. The American social state, he writes in *Democracy In America*, "is eminently democratic" but "not [because] there are no rich." Rather, "wealth circulates there with incredible rapidity, and experience shows that two successive generations seldom enjoy its favors."

The more thoughtful members of this privileged group are aware of this. Nick and Charlie understand that the aristocracy of which they are members is democratic—that is, untitled—and thus they must earn their right to membership in it. Nick's hatred of the titled aristocracy arises not from jealousy but a healthy democratic preju- dice. A more attractive expression of this democratic sentiment is the relative absence of "social snobbery in America" upon which Charlie comments.

The social utility of such a constitution is evident. The danger of falling "oblige[s] members of the U.H.B. to at least appear to act productively and responsibly." In this way, the bourgeois regime— our regime—encourages virtue; it makes virtue the condition for enjoying the most attractive privileges afforded by society. The bourgeois life is a matter of virtue more than it is a matter of wealth.

The requirement that it earn its own way accounts for the contributions to social well-being made by the bourgeoisie. Again, it is Charlie who articulates this idea:

> The term "bourgeois" has almost always been one of contempt. Yet it is precisely the bourgeoisie which is responsible for nearly everything good which has happened in our civilization over the last four centuries.

Charlie's great worry is that the U.H.B. ill prepares its offspring for the test they must pass. He speaks of "'uhb' illusions" as a handicap in the race for success. The illusions to which he refers are the mistaken ideas that a life of privilege might foster in young people, namely, that the good things they enjoy can be had without effort and that their own satisfaction is the only thing they need to consider in making decisions in life. In this view, those who start with little and have to earn all they possess, by reason of this relative deprivation, acquire habits of responsibility and achievement. Their class status educates them to be, in Charlie's phrase, "energetic self-confident achievers." Charlie's insight here is the crucial importance of character. In the absence of good character, all the concrete advantages their parents' wealth and status affords to young members of the U.H.B.—a superior education, access to a variety of social and economic resources, opportunities for good initial employment—have little value. This in turn underscores the importance of the way parents raise their children independent of the advantages their power can secure for them. In the end, individuals, parents and children, must bear the responsibility for their own actions. Insofar as it can, however, by its swift administration of rewards and punishments in the distribution of social goods, the bourgeois regime encourages habits of duty, respect for others, and initiative. In this way *Metropolitan* teaches that this regime will continue to secure a ruling class that benefits society because it makes success conditional on the virtues of practical wisdom and temperance.

On the ride out to Southampton to rescue Audrey, Tom and Charlie revisit the question of Brook Farm. "*Tom:* Yesterday I was thinking. Maybe Fourier was a crank—his ideas are completely unworkable. *Charlie:* Well, I wouldn't want to live on a farm with a lot of other people." Individuals may cease to exist, at least in this world, but political communities are intended by their founders to be immortal. Mere self-preservation may not be the appropriate measure of success for an individual but the inability to endure is a sure sign of failure for a political community. Thus, Brook Farm's ceasing to exist, like the collapse of the Soviet Union in our time, points to a fatal flaw in the regime. The endurance and widespread social prosperity of the bourgeois regime is a proof of its success as a regime, that is, a proof of its justice.

Metropolitan gives this political lesson visual expression in a typically American way. In both the Fowler and Clarke households one sees in the background a bust of Lincoln. The mark of the bourgeois regime's excellence is that from obscure origins it brought forward to govern the nation in a time of crisis the best man of his generation and that, under his guidance, the regime preserved itself and reaffirmed its dedication to its founding principles. Insofar as *Metropolitan* teaches a political lesson, this delightful comedy of contemporary manners reaffirms those principles as well.

Courtesy of Castle Rock Entertainment.

Barcelona (1994)

Six

EUROPE AND AMERICA IN *BARCELONA*

E. Christian Kopff

"AMERIKA, DU HAST ES BESSER!" Goethe exclaimed. For him America was a land free from the ancient traditions that are Europe's heritage and curse. For once, however, the wise German got it wrong. The two continents named after Amerigo Vespucci are dominated by a culture which was imported from Europe and is expressed in European tongues and nourished and maintained by contact with Europe. D. H. Lawrence wanted Americans to turn their back on Europe and embrace Amerindian cultures. Americans of European descent have rarely done so. American religion, politics, literature, and art began in Europe and Americans have returned there to seek the sources of these traditions. Sometimes they stay for only a few years, like Augustus Saint-Gaudens or Margaret Fuller. Others remain, like T. S. Eliot and Henry James, who devoted influential novels to telling about innocent Americans who confront the culture, sophistication, and corruption of Europe.

Dodsworth, Sinclair Lewis's variation on this theme, began as a novel, was then turned into a Broadway play, and finally became a movie (with script by Sidney Howard). *Dodsworth* is not only one of the finest films to come out of 1930s Hollywood, it also gave Walter Huston his most satisfying role (reprising his famous Broad-

way performance). In the film, Mr. Dodsworth is a successful manu-
facturer of high-quality automobiles. His wife persuades him to
sell his business to a larger firm so that they can enjoy the fruits of
his financial success. They travel to England ("Mother England,"
he exclaims as he catches his first glimpse of her from his cruise
ship) and then on to Europe. They find cultured and elegant people,
but also corruption and immorality. The Dodsworths left a hard-
working, industrial America for a Europe that is a playground for
the very wealthy. At first the playground's worst vice seems to be
an innocent snobbishness. The games soon turn immoral and
treacherous, however. Mrs. Dodsworth, captivated by European
society, does not want to admit her age, and this vanity leads her
first into lying and then to worse. Her self-deception and her attempts to deceive others drag her down and threaten to destroy her
husband. He is alienated because he has been separated from his
job, which is his vocation. First his marriage and then his life go
downhill until he meets a woman who teaches him who he really
is and he decides to return to America to start working again.

The protagonists of Whit Stillman's *Barcelona* are young men
at the start of their careers who have gone to Europe to work. Europe in the 1980s, "the last decade of the Cold War," as the opening title calls it, is as enticing and immoral as it was for the
Dodsworths in the 1920s. In both movies, life in Europe represents a rite of passage which teaches the American his vocation
and introduces him to the right woman.

Ted Boynton and Fred Boynton come from an America which is
no longer the isolationist, protectionist haven of the 1920s. America
in the 1980s is the propagator of global free trade. Her fleets and
armies roam the world, opposing communism and defending
America's allies. Ted is a businessman and Fred is a naval officer,
but success for both young men requires a tour in Europe. In
Stillman's shooting script for *Barcelona*, Ted explains the difference

between Europe and America: "This is the way I see it. Work is better in the U.S. Living is better in Barcelona. The question is, what's more important—life or work? Obviously, work."

Ted Boynton is smart. He scored a perfect 1600 on his SATs and got into an Ivy League college. He moved from success in the sales division of his company to become head of its European operations. His hero is the company's CEO, Jack Tyrrell, who rescued the company from ruin. Jack, a war hero in World War II, worked with "Wild Bill" Donovan to found the OSS, which later became the CIA. Into Ted's busy professional and less active social life arrives one rainy evening his cousin, Fred. Fred is a junior officer in the U.S. Sixth Fleet. His SAT scores were abysmal and he went, by his own account, to a "not-so-selective school." After failure on Wall Street, Fred joined the navy (ROTC) and has arrived as an advance man for a visit to Barcelona by the Sixth Fleet.

Success and failure in both career and romance turn on language. So Fred has a question for his better-educated cousin:

> Maybe you could clarify something for me. While I've been, you know, waiting for the fleet to show up, I've read a lot and one thing that keeps cropping up is this thing about 'subtext.' Songs, novels, plays—they all have a subtext, which I take to mean a hidden message or import of some kind. So subtext we know. But what do you call the meaning, or message, that's right there on the surface, completely open and obvious.... What do you call what's *above* the subtext?

Ted answers, "The text." Fred pauses and then proceeds, "Okay. That's right.... But they never talk about that." With this exchange, *Barcelona* invites the modern viewer—so intent on dissecting depth and irony—to pay attention to the value of the straighfoward text.

Jack Tyrrell saved his company from insolvency by reading and understanding the meaning that is right there on the surface, as Ted explains to the attractive trade-show girl, Montserrat. "The truth is that Illinois High-Speed Motor's motors were no longer very fast.

Jack refocused IHSMOCO on what he saw as its real business. 'This means motors and they must be fast,' he would say." Two people understand Jack's point: Ted, and the young head of marketing, Dickie Taylor. Jack plans to turn the company over to them instead of the older people in the firm or to an outsider "with no idea what makes IHSMOCO so extraordinary," as Dickie puts it—because Ted and Dickie understand that what makes the company so extraordinary is a literal reading of its name. It is a High-Speed Motor Corporation that makes fast motors.

Ted's cousin Fred uses language to cover his trail of blunders and faux pas with his vivid imagination, like Mrs. Dodsworth. He invents stories to explain away his past failures and to enliven his present chances of female companionship, never noticing the damage he is causing until it is too late. He explains why he invented a story which sabotages Ted's relationship with Montserrat: "You're in a conversation, it has this momentum, you want to tell the other person interesting or funny things, and you end up telling things that, on reflection, maybe you shouldn't." He tries to impress his girlfriend Marta by telling her that he works for the CIA. When she in turn reveals this to a journalist, terrorists attempt to assassinate him.

George Orwell described the ideologue as a man who thinks in slogans and talks in bullets. The leftist journalist Ramon thinks in slogans, although he leaves the shooting to others. *Barcelona* is punctuated with acts of leftist terrorism which kill and maim Americans. In each case, Ramon explains the acts as "provocations" masterminded by the CIA. As Montserrat tells Ted, Ramon "had read the works of Philip Agee and so was an expert on the American CIA and its involvement in the internal affairs of every country." Ramon's ideologically motivated publication of Fred's reckless boasting leads to the attack on Fred. Ramon's apology is typical of both men:

> I know some people think articles I wrote in some way related to your shooting. I don't agree that a journalist should be criticized for writing articles he believes to be true. But if anything I have done caused you harm in any way [Fred is wearing a patch over the eye he lost in the attack], please accept my sincere regret. If there is anything I can do for you in the future, please do not hesitate.

Fred does not hesitate: he uses Ramon's apology as his chance to get Ramon to help him begin a liaison with Montserrat.

Fred's lying and Ramon's ideological distortions represent the extreme poles of a common difficulty. It is hard to get language to match reality. Everyone in the movie speaks both Spanish and English. Ted even knows Catalan. In practice, however, their shared languages lead to constant misunderstanding. Some mistakes provide the plot's main source of humor; others lead to serious problems, both personal and political.

When Ted and Fred go out the night of Fred's arrival, Fred wears his naval dress uniform. He has interpreted the direct order not to wear the uniform in public "as more of a guideline," since his civilian clothes are embarrassingly unfashionable. As the pair get out of Ted's car, a girl calls Fred "facha." Ted explains that the term is slang for "fascist." "Don't worry," Ted says. "They call everybody that. I mean, you comb your hair, or wear a coat and tie, and you're a 'facha.' A military uniform—definitely 'facha.'" Fred initially misunderstands. "So 'facha' is something good then…. Because if they were referring to the political movement Benito Mussolini led, I'd be really offended." Later Fred gets worked up about the incident ("They obviously didn't mean 'facha' in the positive sense.") and in a fit of patriotic indignation, he tries to deface a wall of anti-American graffiti. While he is doing this, a car pulls up. The trade-fair girls inside, who know Ted, see an American in a naval uniform defacing leftist graffiti. Instead of giving the scene its obvious and correct interpretation, they assume that Fred's uniform is a costume and that they are all headed for the same costume ball. Fred casts aside his patriotic indignation and uses the mistake to begin a liaison with Marta. After they have slept together, she notices that his "costume" has his name in it. "Let me see that," says Fred, who takes the uniform jacket from her and looks at it. "God, how odd."

Confusion and misunderstanding plague politics as well as romance. Ramon has persuaded the trade-show girls that there is an American union called the "AFL-CIA." Marta refuses to believe Fred's denials: "It's amazing the things Americans don't know about their own country." When Ted explains to Montserrat that Ramon is confusing the union, the AF(of)L-CIO with the CIA, Montserrat replies, "Then what Marta said was partly true." In Stillman's script, which differs from the film as it was released, Ramon in the end is wounded in a terrorist attempt on the life of the American consul. Although the leftist terrorists are promptly captured, Ramon's paranoia remains unshaken. From his hospital bed, he asks Fred, "What makes you so certain that the attack of yesterday was not planned by the covert agencies of the United States—or known to them beforehand and allowed to happen?" (The only person in *Barcelona* actually connected with the CIA is the wise, paternal Jack Tyrell of IHSMOCO back in Chicago.)

Misunderstandings affect Ted also. He agrees to go to a jazz concert with the trade-fair girl, Aurora, under the impression that Lionel Hampton will be playing. The concert turns out to feature the Canadian Vinyl Hampton. It is significant that when he meets his future bride, Greta, she shares his distaste for Ramon and insists on using a Spanish word to describe him, rather than fumble in English. Ted understands immediately. Greta, not Montserrat, is right for Ted. She helps him care for Fred and shares his religious inclinations, drawing angels into her sketches. She is immune to the reflexive anti-Americanism of the movie's other Europeans. Ted explains, "Greta's actually looking forward to the eighty channels of television and abundance of consumer products in the U.S. I mean, it doesn't bother her at all."

Ted has been trying to escape the loneliness of life abroad by getting in touch with his ethical, cultural, and religious roots. One night Fred and Marta discover Ted in his apartment, where he is reading the Bible while dancing alone to a radio playing Glenn Miller's "Pennsylvania 6-5000." It is a memorable image of the plight of the American in search of traditions. Separated from his country for business reasons, he dances by himself to the music his parents enjoyed while reading the Bible to make sense of his life. "What is this?" Fred asks. "Some strange Glenn Miller-based religious ceremony?" "No," Ted replies. "Presbyterian."

Fred is also remorseless when Ted complains that Fred has invented a story that Ted wears leather underwear.

> Do you think any even mildly cool trade-fair girl would give you the time of day if she knew the pathetic, Bible-dancing goody-goody you really are? You're far weirder than someone merely "into S&M." I mean, they have some kind of tradition, we have some idea what S&M is all about—there're books and movies about it. There is nothing to explain what you are.

Fred here is giving his negative spin to American exceptionalism, a concept that goes back to Hector St. John de Crevecoeur's *Letters from an American Farmer* (1783): "What then is the American, this new man? He is an American, who, leaving behind him all his ancient prejudices and manners, receives new ones from the new mode of life he has embraced, the new government he obeys, and the new rank he holds." It is this vision that led Goethe to utter his famous beatitude. While it is not true of the American founding, or of American religion, literature, or art, it is true that individual Americans have lost touch with the ancient and European traditions of citizen, farmer, and believer.

Ted sees himself as a traditionalist. A charismatic teacher persuaded him that the businessman's way of life was *not* like Arthur Miller's *Death of a Salesman,* and partly by accident he settled into the sales division of Jack's company. "In sales," he explains, "I discovered not just a job but a culture. Franklin, Emerson, Carnegie, and Bettger were our philosophers, and thanks to the genius of Carnegie's theory of human relations many customers also became friends." The culture of sales allows Ted to make sense of his life but blinds him to the rich traditions and physical beauty of Europe. The most beautiful streets in Barcelona remind him of Michigan Avenue in Chicago.

Ted tells a Catalan businessman, "In true sales you're providing a real and constructive service—helping people make their lives more agreeable, or their companies more efficient, and in so doing creating wonderful economies of scale from which everyone and the whole economy benefit." In Stillman's shooting script, Ted points to the beauty of Barcelona and continues, "I mean, look around—all this, everything we see, was built with sales."

For Ted, one of the most beautiful cities in Europe "was built with sales." This is the innocent provincialism that persuaded Oswald Spengler that there is no true culture in America, only business and material production. Yet the culture of sales gives Ted the moral standards that others find in religion and philosophy. To explain why it is best to tell the truth Ted quotes from his hero Bettger (who is himself quoting someone else, since this is a tradition): "The wisest and best salesman is always the one who bluntly tells the truth about his article.... Being bluntly honest is always safe and best." Fred's lies, deployed to "sell" himself to attractive women, are wrong, and they are not safe. Because of them he is shot and maimed.

Ultimately Ted's intelligence and honesty pay off for him, as Fred's brazen insouciance to the truth leads to his maiming. When the head of marketing at IHSMOCO, Dickie Taylor, arrives in Barcelona to announce that Jack is dying and wants Ted and Dickie to succeed him, Dickie explains to the stunned Ted that Jack never planned for Ted to stay in sales. "You're not cut out for sales—it's not your life's work." Ted objects, "But....sales is more than just a job one's cut out or not cut out for. It's a culture, a whole way of thinking about experience—bringing to bear all the insights of Carnegie and Bettger...." Dickie stops Ted. "Listen, we all like Carnegie and Bettger. Sales is the heart of any commercial corporation.... But have you read Drucker?" Then Dickie gives Ted a copy of Peter Drucker's *The Effective Executive*. It is a book for leaders, and Ted's critical intelligence and honesty show that he is a natural leader.

Barcelona's last scene is set on an American lake where Fred, Ted, and Dickie are enjoying a vacation with their European wives. The girls are eating hamburgers having learned, as Ted had predicted, that European scorn for hamburgers was due to the poor quality of European hamburgers which would wilt before the taste of the real thing. Misunderstandings continue, however. Dickie is with Aurora, but one thing puzzles him. "She keeps asking me about my 'underwear'—and then smirking—as if I'm supposed to know what she's talking about.... What are 'weekends of fun'?" Stillman's stage direction in the shooting script reads: "Fred, surprised, looks at Ted. Ted doesn't seem very surprised." "Oh, that," Ted says. "Montserrat was the same way. Apparently it's some Barcelona girl thing." Fred has suffered partial loss of memory from the shooting and nods. "It does sound familiar."

Earlier in the movie Ted explodes when he finds out that Fred has told Montserrat the same story about him. "Just once," he tells Fred angrily, "I'd like to go out with a girl not convinced that I'm encased in black leather underwear." Fred looks up from his newspaper, puzzled. "That bothers you?" Ted replies, "The exact same story, over and over again!" "Well," Fred protests, "it's not exactly the same. I always vary it a little." Fred's defense is simple. Without

Fred's stories, "Do you think any even mildly cool trade-fair girl would give you the time of day?"

Stillman's direction indicates that this time Ted, not Fred, is the source of the story. Ted has told it to interest Aurora in Dickie, who is a good businessman but boring. Ted then explains the advantages of life with a European. "You see, one of the great things about getting involved with someone from another country—you can't take it personally. What's really terrific is that when we act in ways which might objectively be considered incredibly obnoxious or annoying—(and Fred and Dickie nod), they don't get upset at all, they just assume it's some national characteristic." Fred assents, "Cosa de gringos." As the movie ends, the three men, as Stillman's stage direction indicates, "stand on the lodge terrace with thoughtful expressions, pensively sipping their beers, nodding in agreement, looking out toward the Lake. Inside someone puts on music."

The ending is perhaps homage to the end of Mike Nichols' *The Graduate*, which Fred in *Barcelona* remembers to his cousin as follows: "Katharine Ross has just married this really cool guy—tall, blond, very popular, the 'make-out king' of his fraternity at Berkeley—when this obnoxious Dustin Hoffman character shows up and starts pounding on the glass at the back of the church, acting like a total asshole. Does Katharine Ross tell Dustin Hoffman, 'Get lost, creep. I'm a married woman.' No—she runs off with him, on a bus. That's the reality." Fred's faulty memory omits the movie's last shot. As Hoffman and Ross sit down in the back of the bus, excited by her escape from a conventional marriage, they find they have nothing to say to one another. They stare forward as Simon and Garfunkel sing "The Sounds of Silence." Their marriage will be as mired in silent incomprehension as their parents' marriages, the fate they are running away from.

It is a famous scene, and if "That's the reality," it is a much better argument against marriage than what Fred remembers. In *Barcelona*'s last shot, the European women are inside enjoying their hamburgers and fantasizing about their American mates' sexual peculiarities. The American men are outside, sipping beer and appreciating "what's really terrific" about mutual incomprehension, nodding silently as music starts to play.

Ted's intelligence and his commitment to the traditions he understands, sales and religion, have given him success in business, where blunt honesty and a straightforward reading of the text lead to success. In romance, however, Fred was onto part of the truth. Americans and Europeans—indeed, men and women—can never fully understand one another. Of course, Ramon's political paranoia must be rejected and the cool trade-fair girls must learn to bite, if not the proverbial bullet, at least the American hamburger. They must, however, be allowed their illusions. Illusion, not blunt truth telling, is essential for romance, and mutual misunderstanding can sometimes be a blessing. Ted has learned how to get for himself and his friends a happy ending that combines the best part of America, work, and the best part of Europe, life. For Ted and his friends, Goethe's words are true. "Amerika, du hast es besser!"

Seven

TEXT AND SUBTEXT IN *BARCELONA*

Mark C. Henrie

WE NATURALLY APPROACH ANY work of art through a lens of expectations built up by previous, similar works which together constitute a genre. The success of formulaic Hollywood films is based in part on the satisfaction viewers experience when a film fulfills their expectations: the hero escapes (narrowly), the damsel in distress is rescued, the villain is defeated. While everyone likes surprises, it seems popular audiences don't like too many. The greatest artists, however, have ever been those who appreciate the conventions of a genre and the meanings, moral or otherwise, that those conventions bear, but who are able to alter our understanding—and bring delight—by introducing the *unexpected* in careful relationship to the *expected*. Here is the discipline and the dynamism of artistic tradition.

In recent times, our understanding of the nature of art has itself changed such that engagement with and augmentation of tradition have been eclipsed. Originality has become the key value. But true originality is elusive, and so new conventions inevitably emerge to replace the old. In a critical age, in the age of the avant-garde, older conventional motifs are often deployed, if at all, only in order to be "subverted." And the prime target for such subversion has, at least since Rousseau, been the habits, the pretensions, the prejudices, and the virtues of the bourgeoisie. One of the grand conventions of the bourgeois age has been the bohemian mocking of bourgeois proprieties. Sometimes, this mocking gives way to blistering assault: the much-admired film *American Beauty* traded on a view now conventional among the *bien pensant* that the bucolic American suburb, the very homeland of the American dream, is beneath the surface a weed-patch of pathology. The new convention of anti-conventionalism has thus spawned new genres, each conveying a subversive subtext for the delectation of would-be bohemians. We have become accustomed to reading a work of art for just such a subtext. But what if subversiveness itself were to be subverted? What then?

Barcelona has been Whit Stillman's greatest popular success to date, but the audience to which the film appeals consists, in the first instance, of the sophisticated frequenters of art house cinemas— that is, of those who embrace a cosmopolitan outlook which proudly disdains bourgeois provincialism. That there is a serious artistic intention to be found in *Barcelona*, perhaps even an artistic subtext, is evident in the fact that in video stores, one sometimes comes across the film misplaced in the "Foreign" section, sharing a provenance with *Babette's Feast*, rather than in "Comedy," alongside such fare as *Beverly Hills Ninja*. Stillman knows that his audience will come to the film with certain expectations. His intentions may be discerned by observing how he both meets and foils those expectations.

Barcelona presents us with a tale of two American cousins in an exotic locale during "the last decade of the Cold War." Ted and Fred Boynton are respectively an American businessman and an American naval officer, representing the two pillars of American hegemony: the inexplicable economic prowess of timorous capitalists coupled with the spirited bellicosity of raw military might. The cues are all in order. Our expectation is that this film will follow the conventions of the genre of the *ugly American abroad*. We Americans will be invited to laugh at ourselves, at our naiveté, at our blustering narrowness of vision, at our failure to measure up to the gentle ways of European culture. Or rather, "we" who know better and who pride ourselves on our more-than-American sophistication will be invited to laugh at "them"—those Americans who do not go to art house cinemas, who lack irony, and who take unselfconscious pride in such American achievements as hamburgers and victory in the Second World War.

This expectation is quickly met. On their first night together, Fred and Ted go out on the town. They are American tourists, giving a distracted nod to cultural highpoints like cathedrals and palaces, but becoming more animated when sampling fashionable bars where the most eligible local women can be found: "'Trade-fair girls off season.' Cool. Thanks. This is really good stuff." We learn also that not only are Ted and Fred Americans, but unique for a Stillman film, they are Midwesterners, products of the American heartland. In a sense, Ted and Fred are like the Midwestern deb and her military escort who accompany Nick Smith to the "inorganic" ball, the "International," in *Metropolitan*—"a real relief from [the] hypercritical New York girls," perhaps, but consequently somehow puzzlingly comical in their earnestness.

Ted is something of a prig, a "Bible-dancing goody-goody" in his cousin's eyes, threatened by the powerful emotions stirred up by female beauty. He is also a genuine enthusiast for the culture of sales, with its "philosophers"—Franklin, Emerson, Carnegie, and Bettger—and he affirms that "the classic literature of self-improvement...really [is] improving." The shimmering magical boulevards of Barcelona put Ted in mind of nothing so much as Michigan Avenue in Chicago, which, we learn later, he believes to be the most beautiful city in the world. The more worldly Fred smiles at his cousin's naiveté, since—he asserts as if unchallengeable—San Francisco is.

For his part, Fred is the very model of the American military man in the era of Ronald Reagan. A natural raconteur, he worked on Wall Street before joining the Navy. The Navy was attractive, he tells Ted, both because he couldn't stand the notion of being "stuck indoors for the next forty years, with two weeks off to go snorkeling annually," and because of "all the fighting-for-freedom, defending-democracy, shining-city-on-a-hill stuff, which as you know I really buy." Informed that there is a lot of anti-NATO feeling in Barcelona, he is incredulous: "They're against OTAN?! What are they for? Soviet troops racing across Europe eating all the croissants?" On a public relations mission to prepare for a fleet visit, a mission which will require much tact, he is such an American chauvinist that he expresses his distaste even for *English* accents.

Clad in business suit and naval uniform, these Americans really are what they appear to be. They are, as it were, unadorned, even in their respective uniforms. There is no gap between their "text" and their "subtext"; in fact, they appear to have no subtext at all. And their American simplicity is put into relief in their first encounters with Europeans in the film. On their first night of bar-hopping, a group of young and modish "toughs" wearing jeans and black leather jackets pass by and pronounce the cousins *facha*, fascist. While Fred thinks upon consideration that this was a "close call" which might have "turned really ugly," in fact the "toughs" show no real menace, and as we see with Marta later, the leather jacket is just a fashionable outfit for trendy Barcelona party-goers. Their second encounter is far friendlier, but has a similar point. As the patriotic Fred works to alter some anti-American graffiti with a felt-tip pen—"Yankee pigs? That's meant to hurt...."—a taxi pulls up and three young women emerge dressed as princesses from

Spain's Golden Age. They are friends of Ted's, trade-fair girls on their way to a costume party. The American cousins are bourgeois through and through; Fred's name is even sewn into his uniform. Europe in contrast presents the Americans with layers of complexity. Europe also seems to represent a critique of bourgeois complacency both from below—the radicalism of the anarchist tradition conveyed by the leather jackets—and from above—in the aristocratic tradition of the princesses, which long ago viewed with disdain the rise of the third estate. There is a height and a depth to Europe which makes the middling Americans seem rather narrow.

But then we remember that the Europeans here are *costumed*. They are *not* what they appear to be. Breaking the convention of the ugly-American-abroad genre, our bourgeois Americans have not encountered genuine aristocracy or even genuine political radicalism (yet), only cartoons thereof. Moreover, with their apparent expectation of a gap between text and subtext, it is the Europeans who immediately misunderstand the Americans: the trade-fair "princesses" mistake Fred's uniform for a costume. Something odd is beginning to happen in *Barcelona*, and this peculiarity will grow as the film unfolds. Slowly we may realize that our subversive expectations are themselves subverted.

About the middle of the film, the Boyntons are strolling down a boulevard. Fred, always unsure of his intelligence, ventures a question:

> *Fred:* Maybe you could clarify something for me. While I've been, you know, waiting for the fleet to show up, I've read a lot and—
>
> *Ted:* —Really?—
>
> *Fred:* —and one thing that keeps cropping up is about "subtext." Songs, novels, plays—they all have a subtext, which I take to mean a hidden message or import of some kind.
>
> *Ted nods.*

> *Fred:* So, subtext we know. But what do you call the meaning, or
> message, that's right there on the surface, completely open
> and obvious? They never talk about that. What do you call
> what's *above* the subtext?
> *Ted:* The text.
> *Fred:* (Pause) Okay. That's right.... But they never talk about that.

This is perhaps the controlling passage for any successful reading of *Barcelona*, and it is typical of the way Stillman crafts his art. This dialogue appears at first to have no relation to the plot. It is just chatter a few moments before Fred will learn that Ramon has written him up as a CIA spy. As with the banter in Tarantino's *Pulp Fiction*, it seems to serve merely to delight us with its extraordinary verisimilitude and nothing more. Yet questions about the relationship between what is evident on the surface and what is hidden, both in politics and in love, are absolutely central to the film's concerns. And if we follow Fred's hint and examine the never-talked-about "text" of *Barcelona* rather than scan for the expected subtext, what do we find?

We find that this is a film about Americans abroad, trying rather conscientiously to do their jobs. They confront anti-Americanism, and the military representative of the United States suffers from such anti-Americanism with the loss of an eye. But he bears his wounds nobly (there is no vengeful "eye for an eye") and European disdain for America is gradually revealed to be misguided: for example, *contra* Fred's *bon mot* when confronted with claims about America's notorious violence, the Spaniards seem to be at least as good shots as Americans—and they're far better at bombings. In the end, the Americans have reaffirmed their commitment to American virtues—and in a final triumph, they carry off the women.

Where ironic mocking is itself the point of the ugly-American-abroad genre, in Stillman's film the ironic subtext serves almost as a protective concealment for the provocative events of the text. Thus, whatever we may think of Ted's Bible-dancing Presbyterianism it cannot be entirely "bogus," for we see in the film's "text" that his prayers are actually answered. Fred returns to the living from his deep coma immediately after Ted has knelt in prayer to ask God for his recovery. Well, not immediately. For Ted's prayer has continued, as prayer does, with a request for forgiveness of his sins—in particular his doubting and vainglory—which catapults Fred from the coma to respond, "Oh, give me a break!" In our amusement at the ironic undercutting, it almost entirely escapes our notice that prayer has been shown here as answered. Not only are the bourgeois Americans' political and social values vindicated, so too are their religious values.

On the bohemian taste for a subversive "irony" which is often little more than an indulgence in sarcasm, the film seems even to comment directly. Ted is tense after his date with Montserrat at the Vinyl Hampton concert, and Montserrat notes his displeasure. Ted (rather unfairly) chides Montserrat, telling her that she is "very perceptive," but that he doesn't like perceptiveness "of that kind." Whereas this pretty girl uses "observation for ridicule, as if impertinence were cute and charming," Ted's ideal woman would use observation for "comprehension." Clearly Stillman has, in *Barcelona*, brilliantly observed the language and foibles of bourgeois Americans abroad, and we are charmed by his deft comedy. But we misread him if we take his irony as a form of impertinent ridicule. We must instead follow his observations with a view toward comprehension of the human situation he is trying to capture.

Once we appreciate Stillman's ironic subversion of the contemporary canons of subversive irony, the film's most powerful indictment of the American way of life appears to us in a different and deeply amusing light. Marta has been listening attentively to Ramon, and she explains to Fred why Montserrat must flee Ted's romantic advances:

Ramon is very persuasive and painted a terrible picture of what it would be like for her to live the rest of her life in America with its consumerism, crime, and vulgarity. All those loud, badly dressed, fat people watching their eighty channels of television and visiting shopping malls. The plastic throw-everything-away society with its notorious violence and racism.... And finally, the total lack of culture.

To this, Fred can only respond, "It's a problem." Of course, this is Marta speaking, whom we have not noticed to be distinguished in matters of culture—indeed, she is the least intelligent character in the film, and the most morally compromised. Marta is also a trade-fair girl, and so she is earning her livelihood precisely by introducing American consumer goods, and the accompanying consumerist life-style, into Spain. Like each of Stillman's films, *Barcelona* is filled with characters making *arguments* in defense of their views. In considering the speaker along with the speech, and by relating the speech to the action, we begin to see that the film itself is making a claim. The quasi-Marxist analysis of American bourgeois culture advanced by Ramon (and Marta) reflects a reality, but it is nonetheless flawed—not least because such a view confuses surface and depth, text and subtext.

It is Ramon who has the first word in the film. Examining the face of his new conquest Marta in a mirror, he pronounces it "Perfecto." This same scene is repeated on two other occasions. In one case, with Montserrat—with whom he is cohabiting—his judgment, "perfecto," is met with a question in reply: "Perfecto?" Frowning, Ramon admits, "casi perfecto"—almost perfect. We learn later from Montserrat that there may be something in earnest about the repellant Ramon. He is driven, she relates, by a devotion to the idea of physical beauty—not of flowers, but of the female face and form. "His thought was that beauty is the closest thing to divinity that remains in the modern world. 'All the Old Gods Are Dead'—there is no God, that we know—but in beauty the memory of divinity remains." An old aphorism has it that "Europe is the faith; the faith is Europe." In a "modern world" evacuated of faith, the European Ramon can only commit himself to beauty as his god. And in a kind of aristocratic despair born of theoretical sophistication, he insists that *physical* beauty, surface beauty, is the only true beauty to be found. At least, this is the story he tells to the women he seduces.

Ramon's rival for the love of Montserrat is the American Ted Boynton. We are invited into a comparison of the two by Montserrat herself, who says to Ted, "In truth, much of what you say reminds me of Ramon then." Ted finds the excessive emotions conjured up by the physical beauty of women to be dangerous—to have "ruined lives." With an awkward kind of religious inspiration, he has resolved to go out only with "plain, or even homely girls." So intent is he in this resolution that he actually fails to notice the stunning beauty of Aurora, his first love interest. He hopes to be able to look into the eyes of his beloved one day and "see" her soul. Both Ted and Ramon are driven by a quest. But whereas Ramon perceives the "surface" of things and is committed to the view that (all that is left of) divinity resides in "the pretty slope of an eyebrow or the curl of an upper lip," Ted is not in despair, but *hopes* to connect with a deeper and hidden beauty.

The contrast between the two is highlighted by the fact that on each of the three occasion that Ramon pronounces a woman's face "perfecto," he is gazing at the woman in a mirror. Thereby, the real woman before him is reduced to a two-dimensional image; her beauty is nothing but a surface. With Ted, on the other hand, we see two scenes from his mind's eye, of his beloved turning toward him to return his gaze, a kind of communion. Ramon has resolutely set himself upon the reflection, but the thing itself eludes him. Ted is more of a Platonist. He believes appearances can mislead. He desires to look beyond the image and touch the heart of things, the (divine) soul. Ramon's argument about the disenchantment of the "modern world" seems compelling, but can we really believe that Ted's hope is in vain?

The two rivals have different and equally contrasting views when it comes to the public world. Ramon's political reporting seeks to uncover the secret workings of the American intelligence community—and the political needs of the American president—beneath the surface of events. A disciple of those "masters of suspicion" who have shaped the mind of the modern world, he thinks that the truth of the political things lies hidden below. He is intent on making the events of the day reveal their secret subtexts. On the other hand, Ted, with regard to the conduct of public life, believes in the value of the plain text. Following Carnegie's advice, his straightforward, fair dealing with his clients has turned them into friends. Ted's mentor and model is his boss Jack, "the last of the [American] greats." Jack had himself dwelt in the murky underworld of the intelligence community as an OSS officer in the Second World War, but he returned to civilian life at the Illinois High-Speed Motor Corporation (IHSMOCO, or perhaps IHS Motors). "This means motors, and they must be fast," Jack said. Sometimes the simple text is also simply true. Sometimes sophistication misleads.

There is more concerning perfection. We learn that Ramon suffers from sexual impotence when he has come to know a woman too well. When the "perfecto" comes to be seen as "casi perfecto," when the image in the mirror is displaced definitively by the human being beside him, his love is disappointed. The god has left, and so in time does Ramon: he is a faithless lover in more ways then one. Ted's romantic life in the film shifts twice, again a rough parallel to Ramon. He eagerly attends what he thinks to be a Lionel Hampton concert with the "terrific" but "plain" Aurora in hopes of seeing her soul. He is doubly disappointed: the concert is by Vinyl Hampton, and his companion for the evening is instead Montserrat. Yet he falls in love with Montserrat during a Donna Summers song—or was it a BeeGees song?—and now "everything is different." But in the end, he will finally enter into matrimony with Greta, a dark horse in the romantic race. Whereas Ramon is in quest of perfection in a woman, Ted argues against his cousin, "I don't really buy that, that there's just one girl who's right for you." The deep irony here is that insofar as Ramon directs his quest for perfection to the physical, he is doomed to failure by the passage of time: physical beauty is by nature impermanent, and so, imperfect. Ramon is doomed to perpetual motion in a futile quest. It is Ted's very openness to imperfection in matters of the heart that allows him in the end to enter into the permanence—itself a kind of perfection—of the marriage vow.

Ted is at first concerned with a kind of perfection, however. He wonders if he is fundamentally "cut out for sales," which is to say that he is seeking perfection in the world of work. He argues that "[s]elling is more than just a job one is or is not cut out for. It's a culture, a whole way of thinking about experience." He worries about "wasting [his] life" in an occupation for which he is essentially ill-suited. The happy ending of *Barcelona* is achieved in part because Ted's existential anxieties are resolved together. As he is falling for Greta in the rapid scenes toward the film's end, Ted is also turned on to Drucker, heretofore dismissed as the "cult of management," which will be his new "philosophic" guide as he ascends the corporate ladder at IHSMOCO. His stint as a salesman in Barcelona has not been a "waste": it has won him a bride and a promotion. But maybe sales *is* just a job after all. Surely sales has failed as a "whole way of thinking about experience." For even if Ted's "Maneuver X" works with green carpets, it did not work with love: Montserrat did not cross over the "space" he had created in their relationship. Ted is a failure at "selling" himself when he has followed his professional guides, and yet when he wasn't working at it, love overtook him with Greta.

Fred is a better salesman than Ted. He is in Barcelona as an advance man for the Sixth Fleet, but he also presumes to act in the same capacity for his cousin Ted as well, engaging in a public-relations campaign on his behalf with the Spanish women. He has not read Carnegie or Bettger. Instead, his approach to "selling" Ted to the women is to dissemble about his product: Fred provides Ted with an invented subtext. Beneath his clothes, Fred confides, Ted isn't the "typical American—like a big unsophisticated child"—that he appears to be. Rather, he is an admirer of the Marquis de Sade (and a follower of Dr. Johnson). Fred has more street-smarts than Ted and is more intuitive; he knows more about women's sexuality and he grasps the anti-bourgeois prejudices under which Ted labors. Fred is convinced that given the "Bible-dancing goody-goody" Ted really is, "no even mildly cool trade fair girl would give [him] the time of day" were it not for the fanciful subtext with which Fred invests him. And Fred is successful at first glance. Aurora initially arranges her date with Ted based on Fred's revelations, and Montserrat willingly comes to the Vinyl Hampton concert as Aurora's substitute based on what she has heard about leather straps and "weekends of fun." So convincing a salesman has Fred been that when Ted demonstrates that he is not wearing leather underwear, Montserrat still does not believe him: "So you're not wearing them tonight. That doesn't prove anything.... Maybe they're at the cleaners."

Fred is not above providing himself with a subtext as well. We learn that Fred is reported by Ramon to be a CIA operative because Fred has told Marta during some pillow talk that he is involved in American intelligence, and Marta in turn has told Ramon. Here, as with Ted's putative sado-masochism, Fred has told a falsehood—he was only "joking" in an effort to appear more interesting and attractive than he is. But just as Montserrat believed the story of Ted's leather underwear, so Marta believes Fred about the CIA.

Fred's fanciful subtext in selling himself is what leads to his shooting, and so to the loss of an eye and his memory. Fred's development in *Barcelona* is at least in part his learning to reject his focus on "interesting" subtexts. Or perhaps it is better to say that Fred *forgets* that part of himself which found it necessary to invent such subtexts. He is in the end a convert to the *text*. He has learned from Ted, quoting Bettger, quoting George Matthew Adams: "The wisest and best salesman is always the one who bluntly tells the truth about his article.... Being bluntly honest is always safe and best." Certainly, telling tales about involvement in the CIA is very *un*safe.

Fred has learned from Ted about matters of substance as well as questions of technique. At the beginning of the film Fred is a piratical rake keeping a little black book of information on where to pick up attractive women in various ports of call. He considers his cousin's plan to date only plain or even homely women "pathetic." At the end of the film, Fred looks the part of a pirate with his eye-patch, but he has entered into marriage with the woman he loves. When Dickie Taylor comments that his own date Aurora is "really beautiful," Fred's response indicates his change in character: "I'm not sure how important that is."

Even still, from the beginning there has been more to Fred than meets the eye: or perhaps, strictly speaking, less. He "really buys" the text of the American patriotic narrative, for example, so much so that he is genuinely baffled when he is called a fascist while in the uniform of men who "died ridding Europe of Fascism." Whereas Ted is painfully self-conscious about prayer—religion, not sadism, is his real and carefully hidden subtext—Fred voluntary marks the death of the sailor in the USO bombing with public prayer and does so naturally, without any trace of embarrassed self-consciousness. He simply relies on the prescribed prayer text from his naval officer's handbook. And whereas Ted, in voice-overs throughout the film, demonstrates that he has analyzed himself to the point of near obsession, Fred has not felt it necessary to examine his motives and ends, commenting at one point: "Wow. You've really thought this through. I haven't thought through anything about Marta."

But Fred is not stupid: perhaps his low SATs really were the result of a distracting girl fiddling with her brassiere. It is just that his speculative concerns are less articulate than Ted's (or Ramon's). He is puzzled, but he is not lost. For one, Fred is aware, somehow, of the difficulty presented by the loss of tradition, of historical memory, a characteristic perplexity of the "modern world." Such a concern is unusual for an American, for the United States claims to be the land of limitless self-creation, a land proudly free from the traditions of Old Europe: "It is always morning in America," said Ronald Reagan. We would expect a similar attitude toward the "dead hand of the past" from Fred, but that is not what we find. Instead, his concern is introduced early in the film in an artfully indirect way. As Fred is busy changing the text of anti-American graffiti on his first night in Barcelona, Ted objects, telling him to "forget it." Fred responds: "People have been forgetting things far too long." (He also responds to Ted lividly, "How blind can you be?!" By the film's end, Fred himself will be blind in one eye, and he will be amnesiac—he will have forgotten.) The theme of the loss of tradition is also evident in Fred's recurring quest for the proper way to shave, with or against the grain of the beard. Since his father had never taught him, he worries that he might in time transmit to his son an improper technique. His practical experiments in shaving— empirical science as an alternative to the guidance of oral tradition—appear inconclusive. In the end, the American consul will stand in for the father in passing down the tradition of how to shave. And when Fred's attempt to increase Ted's attractiveness with women by painting him as a sado-masochist is not appreciated, he responds: "You are far weirder than someone merely 'into

S&M.' I mean they have some kind of tradition, we have some idea
what S&M is all about, there are books and movies about it. There's
nothing to explain the way you are." Fred intuitively grasps the
need of tradition, of convention, as a guide in life. But he cannot
quite convince himself that a return to tradition is possible in the
"modern world."

In Fred's early soliloquy in bed with Marta, he notes that "we
almost always assume we are going through life surrounded by
people. Then something happens and you realize: we are entirely
alone." This is Fred's most theoretical statement in the film; its romantic pessimism reminds us of Ramon. But after the "happening"
of *Barcelona*, Fred's shooting, Fred wakes to find himself surrounded
by friends and family who have spent days at his bedside. They
had not given up hope. The note of existential despair at man's
plight in the "modern world" is proven false by Fred's own experience, and he is forced to reconsider what is and is not possible in
our age. Significantly, it is Montserrat who ends up with Fred—
Montserrat, whom Ted has noticed is "very perceptive." (Montserrat is the one who refers to Fred and Ted as "brothers," only to be
corrected by Ted—they are cousins. But of course, they *are* brothers
of a sort, having become blood brothers at "The Lake" as children.)
Fred is blind in one eye after the assassination attempt, but Montserrat can *see* something in Fred to love. Fred and Montserrat can
come together only after Fred's "rebirth" from his coma, a rebirth
which leaves him blessedly amnesiac. Montserrat, recounting
Ramon's theology of beauty, had argued that "in beauty the *memory*
of divinity remains." In Stillman's screenplay, another sentence
immediately follows which did not make it to the screen: "Beauty is
the *memory* of the ideal." Fred forgets much after the assassination
attempt, but he *remembers* first his family—Ted, "the kid with the
kayak only older and fatter"—and he *remembers* his feelings for
Montserrat.

Barcelona ends with a wedding—in fact, it would appear, with multiple weddings, and even with happy marriages. We remember that Shakespeare's comedies also end with such a trope, an affirmation of the gratuitous goodness of human love which, when sanctified, can point the way to the divine. Earlier in the film, Ted had offered cautionary words to Fred about the sexual promiscuity of Barcelona girls: "The sexual revolution hit Spain later than the U.S. but went far beyond it.... Everything was swept aside.... The world was turned upside down, and stayed there." Fred canvasses, with no particular conviction, the line of the bohemian critics of bourgeois convention: "Has it ever occurred to you that maybe the world was upside down before, and is now right side up?" Ted responds, "No, I don't think that's it." *Barcelona* promised at first to follow the conventions of the anti-conventional genre of the ugly American abroad. But the film has throughout subverted our subversive expectations. The subversion is complete with the happy ending in marriage. What could be more conventional, more traditional, than Shakespeare?

In our time, when the reversal of conventional wisdom has become the new conventional wisdom, Stillman has had to work with playful subterfuge, under a cover of ironic concealment, to recover the truth of tradition: this is his brilliant originality. He invites us to *forget* the self-infatuated prison of our theorizing and so to recognize the human goods and graces we really do possess. He invites us to *remember* arcadia ("The Lake") and not to dismiss our longings for a lost communion of souls as mere nostalgia. In the surprising turns of his text, he opens us to the possibilities of human life and love that we had thought no longer possible in the "modern world."

Ramon had the first word in *Barcelona*. An American trio have the last word:

"Cosa de gringos."
"Yeah."
"Fantastic."
"Yeah."

Courtesy of Castle Rock Entertainment.

The Last Days of Disco (1998)

Eight

THE APOTHEOSIS OF DISCO

David M. Whalen

> *From wrong to wrong the exasperated spirit*
> *Proceeds, unless restored by that refining fire*
> *Where you must move in measure, like a dancer.*
>
> —T.S. Eliot, *Little Gidding*

"THE GLORY OF HEAVEN," writes G. K. Chesterton, "deepened and darkened around the sublime vulgarity of man...." It is a long way from Father Brown to disco, but a luminous vulgarity still inhabits the world—or at least can inhabit the worlds created by artists aware of a paradoxical universe. The world Whit Stillman creates in *The Last Days of Disco*—all allusions to Bulwer-Lytton and Pompeii aside—is deeply paradoxical. Widely and rightly ridiculed for its musical vapidity, disco music has come to be associated with cultural horrors ranging from nihilistic sexuality to polyester suits. There are many rooms in the mansion of vulgarity, and one of them is filled with pulsing rhythms and mirror-balls. Nevertheless, Stillman's *Disco* is a microcosm where the discotheque's spinning masses, luminous globes, and dramas petty and profound reflect a dizzying admixture of the vulgar with the sublime.

The most immediately striking thing in that universe is its relentless, delightful, dizzying chatter. It is a world of talk. Strewn
with gems such as "I'm not so much of a bitch as I might seem," and
"There's something really sexy about Scrooge McDuck," or the la-
conically philosophical "For a group to exist, I think someone has
to be willing to admit they're a part of it," the film raises dialogue
to that rare, sparkling level where it almost becomes an independent perfection. Yet it is not independent at all. Poised in and among
the conversational sparks are sophisticated allusions and ironies
that complete the wit of the film. Herpes-infected Alice sheepishly
fills a prescription to the soundtrack accompaniment of "Amazing
Grace." Manic Josh elegizes the transcendent greatness of the (now
dying) disco "movement" while indescribably tacky electronic
church-bells toll in the background. Stillman even indulges in self-
mockery, as when a character from Barcelona speaks to the newly
unemployed Jimmy about prospects in Spain: "Well, Barcelona's
beautiful, but in human terms, it's pretty cold." This is wit indeed,
but it is a kind of wit that at times seems to undermine vulgarity
itself, and slyly hints at traces of the sublime.

As defined long ago, wit is a form of *discordia concors*—the
rendering harmonious of otherwise inharmonious elements. This
definition is itself sly and suggestive, because it may refer to everything from mere wordplay to more complex harmonies of thought
and theme. Among its suggestions is the profound difference between irony and paradox, a difference Stillman both understands
and exploits. As a venerable and potent literary trope, irony's fame
rests on its ability to "puncture," undercut, or otherwise hollow out
a character or idea by juxtaposing it with some kind of negation. It
is the darling of postmodernists precisely because there is (or appears to be) something mildly subversive about irony. It is the most
devious of devices, or so it seems. One catches more than a bit of
irony when, for example, Des McGrath declares that he does not

have to be "some sweaty, horny, hetero he-ape," to appreciate female beauty (and sex). For one thing, this is said as part of his hardly successful attempt to persuade others, and perhaps himself, that he might, after all, be gay. More to the point, the statement is highly ironic in that Des is almost pathologically sexual, a veritable Priapus in the gardens of disco.

Comical and "subversive" as irony is, however, irony too can be "ironized"; the undercutting can be undercut—with paradox. Paradox delves deeper than irony, and in so doing achieves a more profound wit and more meaningful comedy. Paradox undercuts ironic emptiness by revealing that the very thing falsified is, oddly enough, surprisingly true. In the example just mentioned, Des is revealed to be something much greater than a compulsively "horny hetero," and this thoroughly untrustworthy companion is susceptible to far more nobility than some of the more conventionally self-seeking egoists of the film. This does not mean that he is a redeemed or heroic character by the end. His nobility has to do with a higher degree of susceptibility to reality, to self-knowledge. By the end of the film, he is in the way of redemption, though nothing is assured. Yet Des is typical of the paradoxical wit rendered so masterfully throughout the film. The microcosm of the discotheque, for all its vanity, excess, hedonism, and marvelous exhibitionism, contains little explosions of paradoxical nobility, virtue, honor, and truth. And from the funniest sources.

Grace, ultimately, is the subject of *Disco*. Flippant as it may sound, grace is also the film's ultimate form of wit because it elevates the chaos, hell, and even diseases of these searching souls into an experience of something, if not clearly divine, at least ordered and beyond their ability to control. The discotheque pulsates with suggestions of complete human control. The environment is carefully manipulated, and the dancers, as seen from the mezzanine, appear perfectly self-crafted. Many are costumed, and they all seem intent on having a great deal of fun while toying with their own malleability. "Your body...my body," the music repeats, along with an insistent "How do you like your love...?" Everything is negotiable, on the table (or, in one case, the couch), and reality is the stuff of dreams. Charlotte is the dark, pretty, aggressive spokesman for control, announcing early in the film that "this is a whole new era in music and social models.... Look down. We're in complete control." But it becomes clear very quickly that Charlotte is anything but in control. For all her aggressive manipulation, she fairly quakes with insecurity. She makes herself rather detestable early on, brutalizing her quieter friend Alice's feelings by criticizing her for being critical. Apparently trying to "help" Alice with the benefit of superior experience, Charlotte instructs her in the art of control, especially of men: Do not exude the atmosphere of a kindergarten teacher; do not radiate slight yet perceptible attitudes of censure (!); do luxuriate in something—it does not matter what—as being "sexy." Guys really like this sort of thing.

It is easy to see that this kind of verbal pounding is not unadulterated good will. Charlotte is terrified of Alice, for all her apparent social backwardness, as a real threat to her own (Charlotte's) control of relationships. The irony is that Charlotte is actually right about Alice. In fact, for her part, Alice recognizes enough of herself in these admonitions to take some action against them—with fairly disastrous results. But more importantly, Charlotte "ferociously pairs off" with an old interest of Alice's, and as the Charlotte/Jimmy relationship later cools, Jimmy becomes interested in Alice again (to no avail). Charlotte clearly is not in control. Not even of herself. Self-consciously modern and progressive, she nevertheless finds herself longing for something oddly stable, evocative of the old-fashioned and secure: marriage and motherhood (not necessarily in that order). Her desires reach toward a condition that, for all its "security," is not autonomous, in control, or independent in the least. Ironically, she again attempts to secure this new condition through some fairly heavy-duty manipulation, and it fails. In this film, order comes not through control, but through a kind of surrender to what either cannot be or is not controlled. And this surrender operates as a precondition to grace.

Love (like grace) is not terribly cooperative with manipulation or planning. Stillman knows, as did Nancy Mitford, that nothing fails like the pursuit of love. The small set of urban haute bourgeoisie we watch in the film are all, in varying degrees, in pursuit of love, and of the two central women, Charlotte and Alice, it is Alice who partly recognizes that she does not, indeed, control love or even herself. Even while she suspects Charlotte's "advice" as being less than selfless, her desire for love motivates her to adopt it, and this cannot but be comic, and painful. For one thing, Alice intuits that the degree of manipulation Charlotte enjoins is, really, impracticable. But it is worth a try in a world where control seems a common commodity. Though comparatively skeptical and timid, Alice sets out upon a sexual adventure with Tom, a handsome young lawyer interested in environmental causes (proof positive that he is intelligent and sensitive). She returns to his apartment after leaving the disco, and in a magnificently comical scene, labors to belie the kindergarten teacher that she fears lurks in her soul. She fails. Scrooge McDuck is many things, perhaps, but "sexy" is not one of them. Pulsing around the room with automatic hips, Alice declares that she finds Tom's prints of Scrooge McDuck "sexy," and Tom bemusedly understands this signal aright. He invites Alice to his room, and the camera lingers upon her, the bright living room behind her, the darkened hallway before, while she pauses on the threshold. Literally. She crosses it, and the bedroom door closes behind. The next shot shows Alice climbing up the exterior apartment steps in a cold and damp morning, alone.

Alice has succeeded in exerting a kind of tyranny of circumstance (she will determine when and how, no less than whom, she loves), but the romance, so to speak, wears off quickly. First, Tom drops her. In a blisteringly cruel—yet undeniably accurate—reflection upon their encounter, Tom later recounts, "When I saw you that night, you were a vision, not just of loveliness, but of virtue.... You're very sexy and modern and good-looking and hot, but what I was craving was a sort of sentient individual who wouldn't abandon her intelligence.... Why is it, when people have sex with strangers on their mind, their IQ drops, like, 40 points? All that affected, sexy seductress slinking around? Uncle Scrooge is sexy? My God, is there no limit?" Though the cruelty is palpable, and one wishes for a boulder inscribed with "Then why did you partake?" to drop on his head, this is one of those paradoxes; for it is true, and even Alice knows it.

But Alice learns more deeply the mysterious character of relationships and the limitations of our control. People with Alice's temperament actually crave order (dangerously close to control) more than the daring Charlottes of the world, and thus the lessons they must learn about their limits are more immediate. Alice learns that she has contracted herpes and gonorrhea, diseases that effectively wrest much control of her sexual life from her. The utter vulnerability of these young men and women, despite their man-made world, is painfully revealed in Alice's conversation with Tom about the diseases. They (especially Alice) are not sure exactly what constitutes virginity or intercourse. Alice put on a good show of experience, but she now informs Tom she learned such things from books. (Reality indeed.) In a kind of sexual baby talk, Tom laments that she contracted both "G" (gonorrhea) and "H" (herpes) in her first real sexual experience. Darkly comic as all this is, it rises to paradoxical wit as the loss of autonomy is discovered to be the beginning—or at least to allow for the beginning—of wisdom. For as the beautiful-but-not-supposed-to-be-bright Holly tells Alice, one of the alternatives to the current sexual scene "would be some guy so idealistic and in love with you that he'd want to commit himself to you anyway, prior to that step [sexual intimacy], since his dream would be to be with you forever exclusively always anyway." Holly indeed is not that bright, but she happens to be right, and the "stuttering" awkwardness of the last few words takes on, in another paradox, a strange eloquence. Disease actually enables Alice to appreciate the "idealistic" affection of Josh—another character for whom control is dubious—although it is not accidental that Alice takes a detour through the affections of the serviceable Des.

Alice will never develop a new character. She will remain cautious, prone to the reality of books and the desire to control or manage experience. In fact, her promoted status at the end is a blessing and a risk, as it will tempt her to "manage" all the more. But she does learn, painfully, that reality is unpredictable, even dangerous—but also a gift, a grace. It is telling that Josh's vulnerability to manic episodes and his symptomatic singing of hymns is frightening to Alice, yet does not bother Charlotte. Though she is the manipulation maven of the film, Charlotte clearly and accurately rebukes Alice for finding Josh's hymn singing unacceptably weird. "I can't believe how intolerant you are.... Some of those old hymns are beautiful. I've sung them on the street myself; I didn't realize it was so controversial." She then softly begins to sing "Amazing Grace." Charlotte sings from a hospital bed, having seen her own manipulation of (and hopes for) Jimmy fail, so it is possible she bespeaks a tolerance she would have lacked earlier. But it is no matter. Alice is slow to appreciate Josh's steady affection, but she finally begins to return it. It requires a profound experience of her own broken nature to prepare her for accepting something also broken, yet gratuitously good. It is not a matter of physical illness settling for a relationship with mental illness. It is finding the permanent in the flux, the love "so idealistic" in the manic.

Everybody in this film is broken (except perhaps for Van, the disco's own Cerberus), and the Des-Josh-Jimmy trio are no exception. Jimmy is probably the most horrific character in the film, precisely because he is unreflectively self-justifying. Even his self-knowledge (as a failed advertising man) is only about an eighth of an inch deep. Josh, on the other hand, is something of a benevolent oddity. Still waiting to grow into his clothes and subject to episodes of hymn-accompanied depression, Josh is under no delusions of being in control. Not accidentally, he is the most susceptible to gratitude, loyalty, and wonder. He imperils his own job (and later loses it) in order to warn Des that the police are about to raid the disco, and this at a time when Josh and Des are competing for the affections of Alice. It is Josh who has naive faith in disco as a social "movement" ("It's a movement?" Tom responds with bemused incredulity) of those committed to dancing, gratuitous socializing, and exchanging ideas(!). His closing, slightly absurd praise of the now-defunct disco exalts it as perhaps eclipsed, but immortal. As will be seen, there is something profoundly perceptive in this, though perhaps a bit delphically distorted. But of this trio, Des is the most interesting.

Like Charlotte, Des is deeply—perhaps compulsively—manipulative, as his gay-gambit makes luminously clear. The look on his face after he has transformed the ire of an abandoned girlfriend into sympathetic tenderness tells all: he is so amazed at his skill that he begins to half convince himself. Des careens through the film bringing new depth to the notion of being "broken." He snorts the little "gifts" of cocaine he receives as a manager of the disco and even experiments (to our delight) with snorting coffee. His womanizing is compulsive. The height, or depth, of this is manifest when he is caught by Josh "consoling" a woman who represents pure, raw sexuality in her appearances throughout the film. Her name, with a nod to Dante, is Francesca, but she is known as the tiger lady. This "consolation of Francesca" occurs even while Des's interest in Alice is at its sharpest. Des can also be cruel, as when he maliciously publicizes Josh's history of mental illness. Not least problematic is Des's spotty perception of character. Bernie, the corrupt and sinister disco owner, despises advertising people and severely chastises Des for letting his friend Jimmy into the club. In so doing, Bernie quite aptly tells Des, "You've been a good friend to him, Des, but this Jimmy's not a good friend to you. He's out of control. An egomaniac." This is quite clinically true, but Des is blind to it. As so often in this film, someone unsavory may well be the oracle of many truths. Stillman even grants this Bernie a virtue dear to the hearts of many a pedant: grammatical awareness and a love of Hemingway. But this rich comedy becomes more meaningful in the person of the unsavory Des, who remains against all odds a largely sympathetic character throughout the film.

Improbable as it may seem, Des possesses a kind of innocence or childlike naiveté that allows him to deliver perceptive observations even when he is insincere in making them. In one outrageously comical scene Des, Jimmy, Alice, and Charlotte converse in a coffee shop just after Des has been (temporarily) fired. Charlotte quite accurately attacks Des's "pathetic act" in pretending to be gay in order to sever relations with abandoned girlfriends. Des's ensuing hyper-defensive response blends nonsense and accidental profundities. He denounces the "dark side of feminism," where women "have a kind of free pass to make any kind of wounding, derogatory comment [they] want." This is hardly subtle, but his subsequent anecdote—miserably motivated and laden with half-truths as it may be—implies a percipient critique of contemporary sexual protocols. Des recounts an episode in which a Radcliffe girl arrogantly bared her breasts before him, presumptuous, aggressive, and contemptuous in her sexual advance. Josh later confirms Des's story, noting that "he was the victim of female aggressiveness and duplicity—but so was everyone else. Not everyone else then went on a rampage exploiting the opposite sex." Both Des's sensibility and Josh's diagnosis of his reaction to the event suggest a profound disordering of sexuality. Sexual politics or power-play has banished romance, and people become desperately sexual in an ever more frantic pursuit of the "something missing" they barely sense. It is ironic that Des's motive in relating this story is hardly pure or innocent. But the irony is itself undercut by the telling critique implied in the anecdote, as well as the light it throws on Des's own sexual adventures. Nothing is exculpated, but Des can now be seen as one searching, however incompletely, for some kind of love beyond the sex he knows too well.

The meteor strike that concludes *The Last Days of Disco* is twofold: the demise of disco's popularity, and Bernie's arrest on criminal charges. Ash settles everywhere. Josh is jobless because of his "inappropriate" loyalty to Des, Charlotte has been laid off in a merger, Des is of course unemployed, and even Van (Cerberus) has no door to guard. Jimmy has been out of work for a while, and he and Des flee to Europe in the aftermath of the meteor. On the way to the airport, Des reflects on his condition: "I'm going to turn over a new leaf in Spain. I'm going to turn over *several* new leaves." This is a moment of recognition, but it goes deeper yet. Mentioning Polonius' famous line, "To thine own self be true," he wonders aloud, "It's premised on the idea that 'thine own self' is something good, being true to which is commendable. But what if 'thine own self' is not so good, what if it's pretty bad? Wouldn't it be better not to be true to thine own self in that case? See, that's my situation." Jimmy's reply shows up his craven soul (for any who had yet missed it) and is an echo of the criminal Bernie's earlier remark. He likens his abandoning of Charlotte to Brutus's stabbing of Caesar. But like Brutus, he regards this as a "higher loyalty" that makes him, after all, "a good friend to Caesar." Des is incredulous and repulsed by

this self-justifying blindness, and it underscores his own coward-
ice. He reflects that he ought to stay and testify, "But instead, I'm
running like a rat, because 'to thine own self be true.'" This is genuine recognition, though not yet the new leaf.

Des's attempt to flee fails—his passport is confiscated at the
airport—and the final scene of the movie is a kind of denouement
both for disco and *Disco's* central characters. Interestingly, Alice is
not present. She has dramatically "settled out," having been promoted in the merger, and "paired off," having become attached to
Josh. The remaining characters are (almost) all stripped of control
and adrift. They are, as it were, prepared for grace. Charlotte's gentle
rendition of "Amazing Grace" hovers over the final quarter of the
film, endowing it with a haunting sense of forgivable folly. As lives
unravel, the darker, ironic comedy is supplanted by a comedy "sub
specie aeternitatis," or paradoxically divine. Lives are a wreck, so
now they may be rescued. We do not see any such rescue, merely
the preparation for it—though Alice and Josh act as hints of graces
and resolutions yet to come. Interestingly, Des and Charlotte pair
off at the end in a conversation ironically self-congratulatory, yet
again, not merely ironical. "We've got 'Big' personalities," notes
Des. "That's good; the world, frankly, needs more big personalities. But ours burn too brightly, are too big for people with more
normal, healthy-sized personalities like Alice; or abnormal healthy-
sized personalities like Josh; or itsy-bitsy, teeny weeny, polka-dot
bikini-sized personalities like Jimmy Steinway...." There is hubris
and folly in these lines, but he is essentially correct. Alice redeemed
will ever be measured and salutary; Des and Charlotte redeemed
cannot but be spectacular. They are like the "big personalities" of a
Flannery O'Connor tale: the magnitude of their folly is proportion-
ate to the magnitude of their capacity for grace. As Des and Charlotte defensively poo-poo the idea of settling down with one person, they walk off to watch reruns of "Wild Kingdom." Of course,

given the significance of this oft-mentioned television program, this is a rather pointed suggestion that Des and Charlotte are themselves in more danger of "settling down with one person" than they realize. The wild kingdom of human experience may take a detour through simple sexuality, but sexuality too insists on something more. In its integral meaning, it too inclines toward the even wilder kingdom of fidelity, love, fecundity.

Enfolding the noise, lights, failed relationships, and mixed motivations in the film is the sublime significance of pure—what used to be called "mere"—celebration. Celebration has the character of something sublime and gratuitous. It is easy to sentimentalize celebration, just as human vulgarity is easy to sweep under the carpet, but Stillman does neither. In the vulgarity of disco, garish mirror-globed nights outshine "gaudy day." Yet the film itself, through rich paradoxes, hints at sublimity piercing through our magnificent vulgarity. It does more than hint, in the surprising truths and flashes of percipience, in the harrowing of at least some of our follies, in the gestures (and more than gestures) of nobility and friendship. Here, the sublime sheds subtle yet insistent colors over the film, in marked contrast to the glaring non-illumination of disco's spotlights.

Most powerfully, however, the ridiculous gives way to the sublime in the idea and force of dance itself. Dance is symbolic of a universe that is at once mysterious and ordered. Utterly celebratory, dance "trips the light fantastic toe" in an ecstasy of graceful participation in, and reenactment of, this mysterious order. It is our way of hearing the music of the spheres. If disco is an unlikely candidate for making this point, then, well, so is most of our lives. For most of us, most of the time, vulgarity seems all too victorious. But Stillman insists, gently, that ineluctable celebration lies even at the heart of disco. Uniting the ideas of grace and the graceful, or redemption and dance, he rolls the credits to an unabashedly symbolic scene of Alice, Josh, and a subway train full of passengers dancing joyfully to "Love Train." Even those passed on the station platforms are dancing. Then, we hear one last time Charlotte's simple and lovely "Amazing Grace." Perhaps Josh is right; disco will never die. Or at least, a universe with such gratuitous goods as love and loyalty, despite our fumbling, will forever move us to the equally gratuitous celebration of dance. If this seems an unlikely point of view for a sophisticated, contemporary filmmaker, one can imagine Stillman, like Josh, saying apologetically, "Sorry.... But most of what I said I, uh, believe."

Nine

Nature, Grace, and The Last Days of Disco

Peter Augustine Lawler

WHIT STILLMAN'S FILMS, which he both writes and directs, are rather Socratic, Christian, and at least ambiguously conservative. For an audience that for the most part possesses none of those qualities, he presents his insight lightly and indirectly. Only occasionally does he allow us to glimpse the extent of his ambition. He told a *Psychology Today* interviewer that he turned down an opportunity to film *Sense and Sensibility* because he found it unchallenging. But that's not because he does not appreciate Jane Austen's unrivaled ability to discover the truth about human nature or human types in the forms and formalities of her particular class and time. Stillman knows his challenge is to do the same for his class and time. That class was named in *Metropolitan*, his first film, the urban haute bourgeoisie (U.H.B.). Its world is defined by elite New England colleges—Harvard and Hampshire—and Manhattan. The U.H.B. distinguishes itself from yuppies: its members do not define themselves by their professions, and they fear downward far more than they hope or work for upward mobility.

Stillman's *Last Days of Disco* is about the odd and amusing mixture of class-consciousness and self-consciousness of socially, but not extraordinarily naturally, gifted young people in a decadent, democratic time. The members of that class are privileged in terms of opportunities easily gained and in their unprecedented freedom, but they really have not received much of an inheritance at all. Their social position is very insecure. Their status does not guarantee them good jobs or housing, or even admission to their social club of choice, the disco. Their education and breeding have given them fairly good manners and the language and style for clever conversation, but they have not really learned how or what to think about or to believe.

The members of the U.H.B., "uhbs," sometimes speak with an intellectual snobbery that points in the direction of liberal education. A pompous rejoinder in the midst of a conversation about the male view of the female breast is "It is more complicated and nuanced than that." Their higher education allows them to go beyond common opinion to notice that Disney's *Lady and the Tramp* is not really about dogs, because the dogs all "represent human types." In their amusingly erudite, sentimental, and shamelessly self-serving discussion of this cartoon, they cannot see that the types they discover are merely their simple-minded caricatures of themselves.

Their formal education and their tradition have not provided the content required to have a genuinely thoughtful or revealing discussion about human types. Their points of intellectual pride do not take them beyond Disney, Scrooge McDuck, and J. D. Salinger. And with a couple of disquieting, rather disconnected exceptions, they associate traditional Christianity, the religion of their class, with reactionary propaganda and insanity. Stillman shows us a New York full of churches and allows us to hear church bells, just to make clear that the "uhbs" of *Last Days* never really see or hear them—except, significantly, Des. They know of no duties specifically associated with their class, and they are in no strong sense citizens. They really are close to clueless, and they are so insecure or lost in the world that they rarely dare speak of their insecurity.

Because the U.H.B. talk dumb, they act dumb. Their words don't really correspond to their longings and anxieties. Stillman's most troubling—and hopeful—observations concern the disproportion between the pretentious banality of their language and the depth and complexity of their longings. But there is also a disproportion between their bragging about living on the dark side and the tameness of most of their actual experiences and aspirations. These disproportions are the source of much of the film's humor. But we have to listen closely in order to laugh.

In a Socratic fashion, Stillman treats his subjects' opinions, manners, and other modes of expression as revelations of their natures or characters. They may be almost equally clueless, but nature gives them all at least some guidance. As beings given language by nature, the U.H.B. are—like all human beings—singularly perverse, wonderful, and pathetic mixtures of self-consciousness, biological desire, and more. Just beneath the surface of U.H.B. or yuppie uniformity Stillman discovers a fascinating variety of human types or natures. He finds virtue and vice, friendship and betrayal, moral strength and moral weakness, beings capable of loving and being loved (and so of hating and being hated), and what one character astutely calls big, healthy, and bikini-sized personalities.

Stillman's "uhbs" are among the most maligned Americans ever. They are written about by our cultural critics the way black slaves once were. They are called not really human at all. This most damning attack has come from both the Left and the Right. They are one-dimensional (Herbert Marcuse) or flat-souled (Allan Bloom). They are without distinctively human eros or longing. They live contentedly in the present, without God or country or deep commitments or friendships. They are clever animals or competent specialists, and nothing more. They live in an abstracted world created by technology and therapeutic language that has no place for the real human experiences of love and death (Christopher Lasch).

Stillman shows that our critics, in truth, are the ones who mistake abstractions for reality. They write as if the modern conquest of nature has actually transformed human beings into something else, as if Locke or Hegel accurately described Americans today. For the attentive observer, nothing could be further from the truth. Stillman's achievement is to portray the bourgeoisie of our time as human beings. And he does so within the context of a disco club modeled on Studio 54! If there is anything our contemporary culture and critics hold more in contempt than the U.H.B., it is the age of disco and almost all it represents. Disco tunes are often portrayed as soulless and mindless, interchangeable versions of techno-generated rhythm fit for a particularly silly and narcissistic form of dancing in polyester outfits and platform shoes. Disco is denounced because its emergence signified the failure of message-driven rock music in the late 1960s to transform America in an idealistic, ideological direction. To the critics, disco was nothing but a fad so empty it could not last for long. If sixties rock aimed to change the world; seventies disco music aimed instead to divert dancers from the hellish reality that remains capitalist America. The John Travolta character in *Saturday Night Fever* is a depressing mixture of ignorant depravity and misguided nobility, a victim of religious and familial disintegration in an ethnic enclave. He is distinguished from his friends because he really can dance, although he wastes his talent and love of excellence on disco. For them, disco is only opium dulling them to the empty misery of their lives.

Some of our critics do see something good in disco: It was the music appropriate for the wild and impersonal promiscuity of the urban gay liberation of the 1970s, and that sort of mechanical promiscuity, as Stillman shows, was imperfectly imitated by the straights. But surely promiscuity too was a diversion from emptiness, and the illusion of freedom from personal responsibility was destroyed by epidemics of a variety of diseases, most notably AIDS. So all in all, the fact that even the haut bourgeois graduates of our best colleges embraced the disco scene and its music seems to be particularly telling evidence of how pervasive our wasteland was and is.

Stillman reverses the critical ranking of rock and disco. As one of his characters exclaims, disco was much more and much better than Travolta, Olivia Newton-John, and our other fashionable stereotypes. For Stillman's characters, disco meant "the return of clubs, cocktails, dancing, conversation, the exchange of ideas and points of view, dressing up, and manners." Music became less loud and insistent and more melodic and urbane. It made real dancing possible once again, and it didn't drown out all human speech short of screaming. One of Allan Bloom's most penetrating conservative criticisms of rock is its hostility to conversation, and so to genuine friendship. Stillman clearly shares that view, but he goes beyond Bloom by using it to distinguish among, and to rank, contemporary forms of music. Disco, as one of his characters says, really was, for the U.H.B. at least, liberation from the social wasteland of the 1960s, the wasteland which carried over to their undergraduate lives. For Stillman, the days of disco signaled the beginning of what Francis Fukuyama calls the Great Restoration of social life in America.

Disco nights for the U.H.B. of *Last Days* are far from wild or impersonal. They do not dance like Travolta or experiment much with any liberating vice. With one exception, they do not use drugs, and their sexual experimentation is not very experimental. One character claims to be gay, but only as a classy, sympathetic way of ditching girls. Another claims to have gay friends, but we know she is lying too. The "uhbs" seek and find some old-fashioned security in their group social life centered around the Club. The Club is also the scene of intense, college-style conversation, with music only in the background. The Club in effect is college continued, only better. Stillman's characters are liberated from the repressive and isolating ethic of liberation retailed by their professors—and of course, they no longer must waste their nights studying.

One difference between Stillman and his characters is that he really knows and loves disco music. In his film, he allows us to hear almost thirty disco hits, and he chooses them to set the mood for every key scene. The music is more witty, diverse, and pleasing than I remember, and only a very priggish listener could leave the film without seeing some good in it. But the tunes actually seem to mean little to the U.H.B. They only care about having a fashionable place to show themselves off in a well-defined group through talking and dancing. They share that perennial concern with Jane Austen's young characters. They assert that they are less boring and otherwise better than both preppies and the "conceited" antidancers of the 1960s because they really can both dance and talk.

Most of the U.H.B. may not possess the moral strength required for the consistent practice of virtue, but one thing is certain: they are not much distorted by the vice of greed. When push comes to shove, loyalty to friends wins out over vulgar selfishness, although not over attraction to the opposite sex. The U.H.B. are both better and worse than stereotypical yuppies. The Club is a respite from their inability to take seriously what they must do in their careers. When we are shown what is required to really succeed in book publishing and advertising, we have considerable sympathy with their youthful irresponsibility. As a defender of the privileged, Stillman cannot help but have some justifiable contempt for the effects of capitalism on moral virtue, even as he celebrates in many ways the American view of liberty.

The most scholarly of the characters in *Last Days* works in publishing with the two leading women. "Departmental Dan," who has neither the breeding nor the rich parents of the U.H.B., is on the edge of the group. His quasi-Marxist, theoretical criticism of U.H.B. materialism and greed constantly misses the mark, and he cannot acknowledge his own class-envy and attraction to the music and dancing of the Club. He says, "Disco sucks," but he really means he doesn't think he can get into the Club. Nor can he admit or explain his weakness for physical beauty cultivated for its own sake. And despite his knowledge of critics and criticism, he can neither talk nor dance well. The U.H.B. do tend to have the aristocratic shortcoming of insensitivity to their own dependence on the achievement of others and to those not of their class. And they care more about "the environment" or "Bambi" than they do about people who do manual labor. But all in all they are less self-deceptive and more generous than Dan (who actually improves a bit through his contact with them). They see through Dan better than he sees through them. He whines that their criticism is tough, but they brush off his. Class analysis cannot be reduced to materialism, and perhaps the human strengths and weaknesses of one class can rarely be understood by members of another. That is why we turn to Stillman, and not theorists, to understand the U.H.B.

Nature in *Last Days* triumphs in a way reminiscent of Austen: the main characters pair off well by the film's end. Like finally attracts like, and the coming together of friendship and sexual attraction is more important than the fact that all the characters but one are unemployed in the end. Marrying well remains ordinarily the key to happiness in our time, as it was in Austen's, and we can be confident that these "uhbs," still protected to varying degrees by their parental safety nets and now entering the era of Reagan, will make plenty of money one way or another. But we can also be a bit sad at the prospect of the probable narrowing of their social circle. The life of the un-churched bourgeoisie in their prime as moms and dads, married or divorced, in a big American city is ordinarily socially impoverished, or quite individualistic (in Tocqueville's sense), especially when compared to the life of genuine aristocrats.

One of the film's themes is the fragility not only of group social life but of male friendship in the era of the bourgeois or nuclear family. Another is the fragility of marriage in a world so individualistic or unsocial that sex often seems to be the only way really to connect with another human being. Biological instinct by itself points in the direction, as one character says, of "pairing off," but not of pairing off for a lifetime. A third and related theme is the different ways men and women tend to view sex outside of marriage. For women, sex is often a means to security, partnership, and friendship with a man. For men, sex more often serves merely to satisfy the bodily urge and as a momentary respite from anxious emptiness. Women are also capable of employing sex as a diversion, but they are more likely to recognize immediately the futility of the effort.

Men, perversely, are also capable of so spiritualizing or disembodying some women that they can separate romantic love from sexual passion. Men may therefore put women into two distinct categories—the good, or rational, and the hot, or purely instinctual. And they may furthermore view the good as a respite from the pressure put on them by the hot. They may see women as minds or bodies, but not as real human beings: the most pathetic male character in the film is ridiculously disoriented by being unable to see that the same woman might be both very rational and very erotic. All the men in the film are attracted to the one woman who seems most moral or decent, Alice, and that attraction comes in large part from the perception that she is somehow on a higher "plane" than they are.

Men's perceptions are usually too abstracted or individualistic for them easily to have women as friends. Women, clearly, are more social or less individualistic than men. They more readily see human beings for what they are, and so they use their minds less to satisfy their bodies than to seduce men into becoming beings more fit for society. In that respect, as Tocqueville says and Stillman confirms, American women in general are superior to American men in general. We must add that the two successful pairings off in *Last Days* are initiated by men, but by men who had been educated by women. And the earlier, "liberated" efforts of women to control men openly and aggressively fail. It is still the case that the rule of women must be secret and indirect, and that men must be allowed to act as men.

The film's two leading women, Alice and Charlotte, are each a version of the superior American woman. Alice seems at first to be morally superior but practically inferior to Charlotte. She takes intellectual life more seriously, and she is less aggressive and manipulative, more passive about letting nature take its course. Alice wants to trust and be trusted, and she seems to be the mixture of priggish moralism and innocence characteristic of a "kindergarten teacher." She is too judgmental, in part, because she is shy and insecure, and she is readily dominated at first by Charlotte's aggressive self-confidence. Alice wants to be more popular and especially more attractive to men than she was in college. Despite her claim that most young men are shallow "jerks," she is infatuated at one time or another with the film's three most handsome and hardly intellectually compelling men. So she readily succumbs to Charlotte's bad advice to change her image, to become sexually aggressive and seductive, and she has a disastrous (if sexually quite successful) one-night stand with a weak, insipid Kennedy-type. Not only does she give up her "technical" virginity, but she contracts two venereal diseases. The lesson would be the fragility of virtue if we really quite believed that Alice's virginity was mostly the result of virtue. Next she is attracted to a notorious womanizer. Both these men had idealized her, but maybe they had misunderstood her. Her moral decency may have actually been mostly shyness; she had learned how to be quite a lover merely from reading books.

But Alice's experiences with untrustworthy, good-looking men lead her to conclude that "maybe the old system of people getting married based on mutual respect and shared aspirations, and then slowly, over time, earning each other's love and admiration, worked the best." She learns, quite reasonably, to subordinate eros to loyalty and friendship, and so she affirms the "reactionary" view that love, by itself, cannot produce marital stability. By choosing stability, she chooses moral decency, a normal life appropriate for her normal, healthy personality. And so she chooses a basically healthy, competent but not brilliant, admirable, loyal, and devoted man, the "Scottie" dog of *Lady and the Tramp*. Alice recognizes that what she most needs is marital and professional stability, and she finally turns her mind to achieving them both.

But Stillman does not make Alice's choice obvious, because Josh is a former manic-depressive—and so, an "abnormal" healthy personality. Josh realizes that the drug lithium, "a naturally occurring salt," has put him "on a perfectly even keel, perhaps too even." He claims that his first manic episode was not as bad as people think, and he senses that the judgment of others aims to deprive him of something essential to his being. But Josh also says that "I'm still waiting for my 'growing spurt'.... Tall people tend to have great personalities...." He knows he is not "tall" by nature, and the drug has nothing to do with it. Like Alice, he is shy and awkward with others, and he'll never be noticed in a room full of people. He is an unstylish dancer and dresser. In one sense, he has been normalized by a naturally occurring drug, but in another sense, he is quite normal or unexceptional by nature.

Josh's "mantra" while in the hospital for mental illness during college was the hymn "Dear Lord and Father of Mankind." His breakdown may well have been a genuine religious mania, which at

Harvard in our time is viewed as the worst form of nut case. Even Alice is "weirded out" when Josh actually sings that hymn to her when describing his depression and hospitalization, and she dumps him for the moment. Josh was hoping to connect with her on the level of his mania, but he emphatically fails. They never, in fact, connect on that level; there is more to Josh than there is to Alice.

Josh's mania or longing has been suppressed, although not perfectly, by the drug. His devotion to God is partly replaced by his devotion to disco, and he gives a very intense and somewhat ridiculous speech bemoaning the disappearance—and predicting the return—of the good that is disco while church bells are ringing in the background. Josh is "electrified" by disco. But his lithium also allows him to focus much of his longing and devotion on a particular woman, and Alice finally responds to his quite singular love. But we sometimes suspect that she may have finally settled for Josh by denying her deepest, including her erotic, longings. And her success in publishing comes not through finding her "dream book" but by cleverly marketing a fraudulent Buddhist religious memoir as a "self-actualization" book.

Yet there is more to the story, because Alice's settling for Josh is really her appreciation of the genuine good which is the love of one flawed mortal for another. Alice realizes, in fact, that there is something both humanly good and flawed in all that she eventually affirms—her company, which had been "great" to her but downsized her friends, the spiritual truth to be found in the fraudulent memoir, and of course the capacity of the somewhat manic or electrified Josh for enthusiastic and loyal devotion. And the story is more complicated and nuanced still.

For Alice needed help that she could not provide for herself finally to love Josh. Calculation alone had led her to push him away as too abnormal; she really was too cold and judgmental, too intolerant and prideful. The most wonderful part of *Last Days* occurs very soon after Alice hears Josh sing his hymn and right before she becomes certain she has incurable herpes. Charlotte in a moment of despair sings her own favorite hymn, "Amazing Grace," and we hear in the conviction of her voice, and see in her eyes, the joyful help it gives her. We don't see Alice's reaction, but we can imagine it. Charlotte's singing continues as background for Alice's visit to the women's health clinic and the pharmacy. Her knowledge of her incurable disease has made her feel wretched and she appears so to others. A friend lays out her choices now: She can either sleep with men so promiscuous that they are likely infected themselves anyway, or she can find someone so idealistic that he would stay with her "exclusively" for the rest of her life.

At this point, of course, Alice needs Josh like she did not before, and she sees more clearly why he is better than other men in the most important respect. Only the newly but permanently flawed Alice, perhaps, could have accepted the differently flawed Josh. She no longer thinks she is on a different "plane" from him, that she is settling for someone inferior to herself. So as Charlotte says, but for a different reason, there really can be something good about venereal disease.

Incurable herpes, in a most strange way, might have been Alice's amazing grace. Really bad luck turns out to be best for her. It is what finally brings together the apparently healthy and normal Alice with the healthy and apparently abnormal Josh. They both have glimpsed the truth about the human good, including its mixture with all forms of imperfection, in each other. In this respect, we must say that Josh is the exception to the rule about American men. He alone among the men was always attracted to the real Alice, and only for him would herpes (as opposed to a curable venereal disease) make no difference. In this way, he is the most realistic and least romantic of the characters.

A persistent theme in the film's conversations is the extent to which people can really change, or whether their characters are fixed by nature. But a third possibility is a change in a person's nature. Josh changes through the "natural high" of lithium. And Alice changes her nature, in a way, through contracting herpes. But Alice's strange and undeserved natural change is the only one that occurs during the time of the film, and it results in a change in her character. Herpes cures her of some of her pride and leads her to happiness with another. Alice, in her pride, longed for grace less than the other main characters, but perhaps only she receives it. Maybe, because of her pride, she needed it the most. She is grateful to Josh, and not to God, but she sees something of God in Josh's singular devotion, which cannot be explained by nature or biological instinct, much less by lithium.

Charlotte, despite her stunning physical beauty, seems much more unattractive than Alice. She is vain, manipulative, aggressive, completely untrustworthy, and intellectually superficial, preferring television to books. Most striking is her emphatically modern desire to be self-sufficient: "I just think it's so important to be in control of your own destiny—not to fall into that 1950s cliché of waiting by the phone for guys to call. The right ones never do." And she does make things happen; she successfully plans a dinner party in an apartment that she has not yet found. But generally her luck with men is not good. Men prefer Alice's shyness to Charlotte's candid aggressiveness. Charlotte controls her life, finally, by affirming as good whatever happens, however terrible it might seem. She even extols the upside of having venereal disease; it can actually "improve your reputation" with men. In the end, she claims that "[she is] not upset that [she] was laid off" from book publishing, because it "will motivate [her] to find a better job in television."

The root of Charlotte's desire to be completely in control, and so, of her inability to have friends, particularly women friends, is her betrayal by her parents as a child, the typical sort of betrayal in our time. She observes that "people hate being criticized. Everybody hates that. It's one of the great truths of human nature—I think it's why my parents got divorced." The truth is that people hate the truth, and so all must be manipulation. Charlotte usually thinks she has no choice but to live the liberal, therapeutic platitudes of choice and self-sufficiency because love is an illusion and other people will invariably betray you. She views compulsive betrayals and cruel candor as preemptive strikes, and her talk about control barely conceals how chaotic or out-of-control her soul really is. Her deeper aim is longing to achieve an "emotional breakthrough" with a man, and she breaks down when her best effort fails. Her deepest suspicion is that for some cruel reason that possibility has been denied her.

Charlotte, the big, "television" personality, is surprised by how "intolerant" Alice is about Josh's hymn-singing. She says, "I've sung [hymns] on the street myself—I didn't realize it was so controversial." And she is not just once again asserting her superiority to Alice. She sings "Amazing Grace" quite movingly. It is a sign of her (quite temporary) loss of personal control. It may also be a sign that she is deeper and less normal than Alice or the lithium-dosed Josh. Charlotte, we can say, knows—at least sometimes—that the view of life she voices is untrue, and her personality is large enough to reach beyond the banalities of her time and class. She knows on occasion that she needs help she cannot provide for herself. She knows that she is a soul in trouble and somehow in need of grace. Liberal, individualistic extremism points not to bourgeois self-sufficiency but to a return to faith. And Charlotte's experiences, far more than Alice's, constitute *Last Days'* criticism of the misanthropic pretensions of feminism.

Charlotte ends up with Des, the only character, at first, who seems worse than she. He is a Harvard dropout, a nightclub "flunkey," a promiscuous coward with women, a cocaine addict, and generally irresponsible. His constant theme is *change*. Sometimes he asserts he can change even his sexual orientation to suit his convenience. He hopes that the influence of a good woman like Alice, combined with the institution of marriage, can change his womanizing ways. And he resolves "to turn over a new leaf" or "several new leaves." Most of his talk about change comes from weakness of will; he won't really make the effort to change. But he is not wrong to think that he is morally weak by nature, and he often recognizes his sins for what they are. He criticizes "the Shakespearean admonition 'To thine own self be true,'" asking "What if 'thine own self' is not so good—what if it's pretty bad? Wouldn't it be better not to be true to 'thine own self' in that case? You see, that's my situation." But in truth, that is the situation of all human beings, and "To thine own self be true" is the cliché at the heart of the American lie of self-sufficiency.

So Des has a sort of self-knowledge that is more Christian than is the quest for self-actualization. He sometimes knows, more than Alice did, that he needs to change, and that his weakness of will makes change impossible without help beyond the self. He knows, like Charlotte, that he needs something like grace, or at least an extraordinary and undeserved woman. And at the film's end he experiences a genuine kinship with Charlotte. They make a date to watch TV. Des knows that Charlotte can see through him. They can see through each other—and so appreciate the strengths and weaknesses, the greatness and the misery, of each other's big personalities. Their screwed-up lives make clear the looniness and the deprivation at the heart of bourgeois life, and even at the heart of human life. So their natures and their need for (and so, perhaps, open-

ness to) grace, the unexpected intrusions of Christian anthropol-
ogy into the closed world of the U.H.B., is Stillman's message of
hope.

Perhaps the end of disco is also the end of the U.H.B., that
partly aristocratic class that is better and worse than yuppies. Alice
and Josh are likely on the way to becoming yuppies, although yuppies of the most decent and admirable sort. Charlotte and Des may
well have big careers in television and nightclubs, but in those
fields the size of one's personality transcends class. Stillman's sympathy for his characters is evident in his own choice of the big
adventure of filmmaking over the security of a salaried job, and in
his awareness of his own natural excellence. Stillman remembers
the U.H.B., but he is no longer one of them. None of the U.H.B. has
many resources from the past on which to draw, and so their fu-
tures, as one character says, will largely be determined by how
well their natures fit the contexts in which they find themselves.
Natural flourishing depends quite a bit on luck, and nature cannot
be completely mastered or brought under control. So there is still
space or need for grace—a grace which may mysteriously appear.
The film ends with Alice and Josh dancing on a train to the feel-
good disco hit "Love Train." Love has made them happy enough in
a quite healthy and normal way. But the final song of the film, sung
over the credits, is Charlotte's "Amazing Grace." Nature is not quite
enough to account for human experience, and, by itself, nature is
not what makes possible human change or conversion.

METROPOLITAN

Luc Sante

IN THE WORLD DESCRIBED by the movies today, the American aristocracy is something like the vermiform appendix: it persists vestigially, if it persists at all. This is more a reflection of prejudice and myth than of any truth. America wishfully thinks of itself as a classless society, and old money assists this illusion by concealing itself and shunning anecdote. Whit Stillman's *Metropolitan* is, therefore, one of the year's most daring movies simply by virtue of its subject matter. When I told friends that I had been to a screening of a very good film about debutantes and their dates, I met with reactions that ranged from incredulity to derision to hostility. I invariably fell back on analogy: imagine a movie about the social life of the Bayaka Pygmies, told from their own perspective.... People were then generally willing to grant it anthropological value.

But *Metropolitan* is more than a curiosity. It is funny, moving, and entertaining, boasts a wonderful cast of unknowns, and ties a bunch of divergent formal strains into a seamless whole. The story takes place in New York during Christmas vacation, a hectic time filled with gala soirees. In the center of the composition is a group of friends who call themselves the Sally Fowler Rat Pack, after one of their number who hosts the post-dance skull sessions that supply the setting for much of

This article originally appeared in *Wigwag* (October 1990).

the picture. As the movie begins, the seven members annex an eighth, a lone wolf named Tom Townsend, to even the gender balance in the face of "a severe escort shortage." Tom acts as both the story's catalyst and the audience's knot-hole viewpoint.

The Rat Pack is composed of a delicately varied assortment of personalities. Sally Fowler herself is somewhat recessive at first, but comes to reveal smoldering ambition. Fred Neff is usually either dazed or asleep, but he, too, has a hidden, rather mordant self. Jane Clarke aspires to life as a queen bee, and possesses a gravity that makes her seem older than her friends. Cynthia McLean is sensual and capable of treachery. Charlie Black is bespectacled and fond of making pronouncements; he might grow up to be a conservative newspaper columnist. Audrey Rouget is a sensitive soul who is learning about life by reading classic novels. Nick Smith, the pack's real leader, is impulsive, highly verbal, apparently superficial but unexpectedly profound. Tom Townsend, as the protagonist, is the figure who sets himself slightly apart from the crowd, the insecure rebel and proudly hesitant candidate for membership.

Tom is, in fact, whether he likes it or not, not quite one of them. His parents are divorced, and even though he comes from the right background, he now lives in the nether land of the West Side with his mother, who has no money of her own. Thus, he spends a lot of time concealing his deficiencies—that his tuxedo is rented, for example, or that he wears a raincoat because he can't afford an overcoat. Idealism and defensiveness both show up in his gloriously ill-founded but well-meant espousal of the utopian social theories of Charles Fourier. The story gets rolling as Audrey falls in love with Tom, which prompts him to resume actively his dormant infatuation with the impossibly distant Serena Slocum. The narrative assumes its full shape with the incursion of a classic bully, Rick von Sloneker, whose every move appears to be in furtherance of some dark design.

Like its progenitors in that nearly extinct category, the well-made film, *Metropolitan* plants one foot in archetype and the other in reality, with somewhat more weight on the latter. Its literary forebears are even more in evidence. Tom Townsend is unmistakably the offspring of F.

Scott Fitzgerald's sincere young heroes, although the world he enters is more closely knit and more fundamentally provincial than Fitzgerald's haut monde. It is, in fact, a fishbowl out of Jane Austen. None of these allusions are concealed by the director, who also wrote the script. Austen is invoked frequently, but Stillman manages not to make it seem coy when (for example) Tom and Audrey argue about the "immorality" of the young players in *Mansfield Park* (Tom, characteristically, has not read the book but relies on Lionel Trilling's account of it, insisting the critics get to the heart of the matter and spare the reader needless toil). Like Austen, Stillman wears his irony lightly and deploys it by degrees, savoring a pattern of pas de deux interspersed with full ensemble numbers.

The look of *Metropolitan* derives from a very different tradition, in part because the film was made on a tiny budget that restricted locations and virtually precluded camera movement. Stillman and his gifted and resourceful cinematographer, John Thomas, worked out a series of graceful compromises, between stasis and airiness, formal composition and liquid spontaneity. The result is a look, surprisingly apt, that is most reminiscent of the early films of Eric Rohmer, and the disarmingly daffy end sequence has a low-budget, the-hell-with-it rambunctiousness that evokes Godard's *Band of Outsiders*. Does any of this seem odd in a movie devoted to the urban haute bourgeoisie?

Well, maybe, at first, but its internal logic is convincing. "Urban haute bourgeoisie," or U.H.B., is a term coined by Charlie, who is obsessed with the imminent doom of his class. Stillman views this ironically, of course, beginning with the film's title, which is tongue-in-cheek in its irrelevant grandeur. Charlie, pining hopelessly for an era of civic responsibility and disinterested paternalism, is just one of the author's masks. Tom, half pledge and half Decembrist, wanting both to join the party and to dismantle it, is another. Nick, just as game to fight a duel as to participate in a déclassé nationally televised ball featuring debs from the boondocks and a complement of military school escorts, is yet a third.

The female characters are less opinionated but no less central, or no more off-center. Audrey may possess the substantialness of her class but she has none of its self-confidence. Jane has all the moves down, but they barely conceal a basic trashiness. Cynthia's vulgarity is the sort that can come only from a deeply rooted sense of privilege. Sally has been endowed with all the poise and decorativeness that breeding might confer, and she wants to be a pop star. No differently than Tom, each of the characters is attempting to straddle opposing sets of values. Stillman only becomes explicit about his point of view in one scene not far from the end. Tom and Fred are in a bar with Charlie, who has just delivered the eschatological sermon on class to which he has been building up. They spot a fellow in his late thirties, and Charlie looks to him for confirmation of his theory. The graybeard doesn't laugh or walk away, but says, in effect, Just get on with things. The point is clear, if unresounding: realism and compromise are the necessary tools for survival.

This may sound dully practical, but the story's unforced symmetry and the characters' very credible complexities fill it out beautifully, and the movie's plasticity makes it even seem adventurous. Form really does follow function in this film; its classicism is appropriate to the foundations of the class it depicts, while its New Wave elements reflect the destinies of the individual characters. No less than any of the 1959 breakthrough works of the *Cahiers du Cinéma* crowd, *Metropolitan* is a triumph of slap-up improvisation over limited resources, and it tells a story that echoes that of its own construction: it is about making do. The notion that these defenseless members of a dinosaur class will be left to pick their way through the gutters of the world might sound like special pleading. The movie certainly does not concern itself with political questions—the money and the power that lurk behind all the cultural anxiety and ritualistic tinsel of the upper bourgeoisie go unmentioned—but it is, after all, a movie about kids.

The single most remarkable thing about *Metropolitan* is the level of the acting, both individually and as an ensemble. The star is Christopher Eigeman, a dazzling actor who is consistently fun to watch, so that it is a major letdown when Nick disappears for unsatisfactory plot reasons about two-thirds of the way through the picture. Carolyn Farina, as Audrey, has a fine delicacy of manner, and Taylor Nichols is creepily convincing as Charlie. We will undoubtedly be hearing from all of these actors again before long.

Places in the Heart

Donald Lyon

> I believe in the detached approach for comedy. If
> you really look at anything, there's always a
> comic note. A painful one, too. One brings the
> other to life.
> —George Cukor, in *Cukor on Cukor*

WHIT STILLMAN'S FIRST FILM, *Metropolitan*, was a mock-anthropo-
logical look at a tribe—puppy socialites in New York—that had evolved
a language too baroque to cope with the emotional realities of its life. His
second film, *Barcelona*, is a comedy of cultural misreading in which two
late-twenties Americans abroad in a magical place make blunder after
blunder. The locale is Barcelona, a city that has played a key role in
Stillman's professional life. Ted is running the foreign sales office of a
Chicago firm; his cousin Fred, a Navy lieutenant, arrives in the Catalan
city to do P.R. work for an upcoming visit by the U.S. Sixth Fleet and
plants himself in Ted's apartment. The time is, precisely, "the last decade
of the Cold War" and Barcelona is rife with anti-Americanism.

Both guys make mistakes about their jobs: Ted is convinced that he
is "not cut out for sales" and that he is about to be fired. Fred's obnoxious confrontational personality decides the best way to deal with political animosities is to flaunt his Yankeeism: he insists on wearing his uniform in public. ("Men wearing this uniform died ridding Europe of fascism," he pompously remarks when he hears himself called *facha* in the
street—he repeats the line proudly later, but then admits he has no other
clothes.) He tries to liven up a boring local party with a limbo contest.

This article originally appeared in *Film Comment* (1994), 82-84.

With a felt-tipped pen, he alters a graffito about Yankee "pigs"—*cerdoes*—
to Yankee "deer"—*ciervos*. ("I don't think 'Go home, Yankee deer' is
much of an improvement," says his cousin.) He belligerently defends our
Vietnam policy with a simile about red ants that offends a gathering of
intellectuals. (Ted: "You confirmed their worst assumption"; Fred: "I *am*
their worst assumption.")

And they make romantic miscalculations: Ted, after a heartbreaking
relationship that was, he assures us, "carnal," vows he'll now fall for
only plain women but promptly tumbles for a blonde beauty, Montserrat, while disco-dancing to what he misidentifies as a Donna Summers
song. This is not the last step, naturally, for Montserrat is (a) still quasi-
involved with a womanizing anti-American journalist and (b) the object
of Fred's desire, too. Both men are caught up in a rondo of missteps.
They are both ungainly but eager disco dancers; predictably, the one
graceful, harmonious dance moment in the movie shows its four principal women flamencoing by themselves on a patio, watched by the guys.

As *Metropolitan* made clear, Stillman loves to exaggerate the talk, to
heighten the rhetoric of his sample group to the edge of parody; in this,
if in little else, he resembles Tarantino. Here, at the start, serious Ted riffs
about pretty vs. homely girls; Fred indulges in a long spiel about techniques of shaving; Ted will, at a moment of emotional crisis, solemnly
tell his cousin that the lyrics to popular songs are our guide to romance.
Fred's defensive jingoism comes out in an analysis of Euro-hamburgers
and an attack on one of the Spanish words for Americans—
"*Estadunidense*"—because of what he reads as the contemptuous "dense"
in its last five letters. All this has the effect of totally ironizing the heroes;
everything about them is, at best, likably ridiculous, as when Ted, alone
in his apartment, guiltily pulls out from behind the cover of an *Economist*
an Old Testament and reads it silently while doing a solo lindy-hop to a
recording of Glenn Miller's "Pennsylvania 6-5000." In voice-over, mean-
while, he meditates on the nature of goodness (is it to "stop doing harm"?).
But then, Ted always makes a musical fool of himself: Fred walks in on
him during Glenn Miller and later calls him a "pathetic Bible-dancing
goody-goody"; he gets that disco tune wrong; he thinks at one point

he's going to a Lionel Hampton concert, but it's somebody called Vinyl Hampton who turns out to be playing.

The film's very grammar conspires to mock him: at least twice, we get to see his dream image of a woman he expects to find awaiting him at an encounter, only to be disappointed by the woman in reality. And Barcelona itself, as John Thomas, the cinematographer also of *Metropolitan*, shoots it, serves as a cool green space calculated to put Ted and Fred in their place. In a typical visual trope, Ted is heard in voice-over moaning about how he's going to be canned and *then* we glimpse him standing rigidly at a desk, phone in hand, in a richly brown art-nouveau office whose curvilinear decor mimics the twining tendrils of growing things and mocks the yuppie anxieties of the uptight Yánqui. It's not surprising that Stillman, wary of clichés, includes not a single shot of a signature Gaudí building in this valentine to Gaudí's city—in this respect unlike that other recent tribute to the city, *The Hours and Times*.

What does this delicate but relentless tone add up to? What is Stillmanian irony? It is an irony that walks a tightrope between affection and satire. For affection, take *Four Weddings and a Funeral*, where director Mike Newell, writer Richard Curtis, and actor Hugh Grant all cooperate in sustaining an attitude of adoration for the articulate charm of Charles. *Four Weddings* is a clever and likable romantic comedy, but it takes no real risks and courts a certain smugness, even to its echo of the plot of *The Graduate* at the end. (*The Graduate*, incidentally, comes up in *Barcelona* when Fred gloomily warns Ted that his upcoming wedding might turn out like the one in that movie.) For satire, take *The Hudsucker Proxy*, where the Coens use everything—space, lighting, movement, lens, clothes, color, language—joylessly to belittle the pathetic energies and egos of those roaches, their characters. (To think that Billy Wilder was once accused of "superficial nastiness" and of "brutaliz[ing] charming actresses.") Compared to these filmmakers, Stillman's handling of his central figures is morally complex. For instance, Ted's Bible-reading lindy-hop is both foolish and not foolish, both a parody of Puritanical self-absorption and a real reach for grace.

Too, there run throughout the film references to the language of self-help business-babble books such as those of Dale Carnegie and Frank Bettger; this language is both teased and not teased. There is a wonderful flashback consisting of two shots: a scene from a school performance of *Death of a Salesman* that had turned Ted against business and a classroom shot of a charismatic business prof who reoriented him businesswards. Stillman is from one angle the artistic lovechild of Jim Jarmusch and Philip Barry—half affectless recorder of pointless effort, half laureate of success.

But Stillman in *Barcelona* challenges himself a bit. He imports, as Cukor recommends, pain. Stillman said that he wrote *Metropolitan* under the conviction that "life is essentially an eventless affair and to make a movie full of plot and incident would be a false and inauthentic repetition of genre movie clichés. In the interval between the two scripts I changed my mind: life does have melodramatic turns...."

There are three violent acts in the film, successively more implicating. Almost the first shot is of a bomb exploding harmlessly at the American Library. Later, a sailor is killed by a bomb at the USO and Fred, in uniform, reads the Burial at Sea in a dockside warehouse and passes a bottle of purloined scotch to the sailor's buddy, who says his friend wanted to be the "Brooklyn Johnny Cash." We see most of this from a truck approaching to hoist off the coffin. The scene edges close to contempt, but is saved by a Hawksian avoidance of maudlin emotion in the guys (faint echo of *Only Angels Have Wings*). Thirdly, there is Fred, who has refused to soft-peddle his patriotism or to abandon his uniform. Ted scoffs at Fred's feeling he's being followed and the cousins have a nasty fight about money. Then Fred, after finding out his girlfriend is larcenous and unfaithful, is riding in a taxi grimly repeating a mantra from Dale Carnegie: "Every day in every way I am becoming a better Lieutenant Junior Grade," when a scooter pulls up alongside and its passenger shoots him.

There then ensues an agonizing bedside vigil by Ted—both a purging test for Perceval and a parody of such an ordeal, as was, in a lighter and less risky way, the "rescue" attempted by the hero at the end of *Metropolitan*. Ted's first thought, in voice-over, as he races into the beautiful art-nouveau hospital where Fred lies in a coma, is a classic piece of Protestant self-reproach to the effect that even disasters reach us through our own colossal egotism. He reads *The Scarlet Pimpernel* to his coma-tose cousin and has visitors spell him with readings of *War and Peace*—the two books a nice contrast of period camp vs. period nobility. At bedside, he flashes back to "The Lake," where at age ten, the cousins blood-bonded while fishing and fell out over a kayak Fred stole and sank. He kneels and prays with the amazing persistent visitor and sketcher Greta ("Do you know any Catholic prayers?" he asks). Finally, he con-fesses remorsefully that he never until now believed that Fred got low SAT scores only because he was distracted by a girl's unbuttoned blouse. At this very point, Fred's eyes pop open and he returns to consciousness with the words, "Give me a break"—another Hawksian deflection of sentimentality. "This means a complete and total recovery," beams Ted, delighted to witness the rebirth of his cousin's obnoxious acerbity.

This uncomplaining facing of pain, accompanied by no political re-criminations from the two Americans and later grace-noted by a more-than-accepted apology from the anti-American journalist, somehow purges the cousin's callowness and readies them to join in a happy, harmonious finale out of Shakespearean romantic comedy. The valley of pain traversed, all things fall into place: Ted gets not a dismissal but a promotion (but back in Chicago), and he has found true love not in the elusive blonde Montserrat but in the persistent Tolstoy-reader, Greta. Which leaves Montserrat free for Fred. A smiling sextet of three Ameri-can men and three Catalan women are grilling and sampling big, deli-cious-looking hamburgers back in the U.S., at The Lake. This ham-burger-validation hits a complicated, and always-comic, note. The film, which has not been shy about showing the arrogant bumptiousness of fatuous Yánquis, earns this moment of beef pride. The guys grill the burgers, and the women go off laughing about the guys; the guys ac-cept, indeed rejoice in, the women's impenetrable amusement about their "cosas de gringos."

Barcelona is totally a guy-o-centric movie in structure: the point of view is mainly Ted's; Ted gets the voice-over; Fred is occasionally seen away from Ted but never gets a voice-over. The film's women are present only in relation to the men, just as men are never shown in Jane Austen outside the company of women. The differences between genders are exaggerated here—not only the obvious American-Catalan divide, but Ted and Fred are both earnest, monogamous romantics, while blonde Montserrat and dark Marta (Greta is a very late arrival) are both coolly liberated polygamists. This is the wild Spain that Stillman calls "Early Almodóvar." Stillman as artist is clearly of the Ted/Fred persuasion regarding sex; he has actually admitted, "I don't really like the idea of characters actually touching in a movie. I thought maybe the characters could talk in bed, as if they had just woken up from a nap or something; naps are really necessary in Barcelona." Sure enough, he cuts a couple of times from disco-dancing to two talking heads in bed, and the heads are talking at total cross-purposes. Ted is allowed one kiss (it was a last-minute Stillman decision and had to be shot at the cast party); it is with, natch, the wrong girl.

What's remarkable here, though, is that for all Stillman's shy or delicate or fastidious refusal to appropriate the feelings of the film's women, there is communicated a warm sense of their cheerful, smart existence going on out of the range of the camera. Far from being judged by Ted/Fred standards, they wise up Ted/Fred and the movie itself. For all the male verbalizing and strategizing about *l'amour*'s maneuvers, it is the women who end up authoring the script. This is due, of course, to the lovely playing of Tushka Bergen as Montserrat, Mira Sorvino as Marta, and Hellena Schmied as Greta. Ted and Fred are Taylor Nichols and Chris Eigeman, both familiar and familiarly articulate from *Metropolitan*; both resolutely refuse to charm—which is the ultimate key to charm. We leave *Four Weddings* thinking no one could possibly be so debonair as Charles and looking for warts; we leave *Barcelona* thinking, Yeah, I know, wonk assholes...but I can't help liking them.

Stillman is, for all the eloquence of his surface and the eloquence of his chatter, an elusive, enigmatic filmmaker. He seems possessed by rigorous moral reticences: skeptical of incident in narrative, he is both prodigal of words and dubious about their validity. He brings a (perhaps secularized) Protestant suspicion of emotional indulgence not wholly unlike Godard's paring rigor. He exhibits, too, a talent and an eagerness to have his people talk through the big and little things of life and love that is not wholly unlike Rohmer's. The brilliant *Barcelona* shows, in its greater richness than that of *Metropolitan*, the kind of growth we always hope for in a major artist. *Barcelona* marks a twofold advance: it incorporates pain into the Stillmanian world, and it knows how to counterpoint glib verbal certainties with beautiful ambiguities of image and framing (the camera rarely moves). Barcelona was a Puritan paradise for Stillman, clearly, and he makes us savor how places—not necessarily Barcelona, but wherever—can enchant, liberate, inform. The film ends with the little boys fishing and the limbo song rising on the soundtrack—as if to hold in perpetual tension the dialectic between paradise and home.

CALL IT COSMOPOLITAN

Armond White

WHIT STILLMAN EMBARRASSES white critics who don't like to be reminded what social group they belong to, or which class categories exclude them. It's comical—almost as funny as Stillman dialogue—to see them knock *The Last Days of Disco* because it isn't about black and gay subcultures (like they care) or Studio 54 in its prime. Read the title, kids.

The subject of Stillman's three films so far is white insularity—a commonplace that goes unquestioned, in fact celebrated, in most American movies. But not here; implicit in Stillman's *Disco* is a rare, rueful knowledge of white cultural succession. Set in the very early 1980s, *Disco* captures a particular moment—after disco's heyday but before the yuppie coronation became official. Stillman's tiny world affords the most accurate-yet view of that subtle social transition (as smooth as the chord changes in "Good Times," but not as beneficent). This may frustrate people who want to see guiltless urban glamour plus the rush of a hectic environment and gaudy atmosphere. The latter seems outside Stillman's temperament yet his language and plotting are nuanced and evocative. True to psychological convolutions that occur within fad and trend, he isn't just partying, but has made a serious comedy.

Stillman follows a group of Harvard grads and boarding-school girls laying claim to New York City as a birthright. Entry-level publishing grunts Alice and Charlotte are man- and career-hunting. At a Studio 54-like club, they intermingle with Josh, an assistant district attorney; Jimmy, an ad man; Des, the club's major-domo; plus Dan their publishing coworker. Stillman gets the personalities as correct as the chronology. These horny

This article originally appeared in the *New York Press* (1998).

stiffs are not chic socialites or that later grungy phenomenon, Club Kids; inheritors and despoilers of urbane leisure, these in-between elites, in fact, pioneered the 1980s déclassé nightlife (soon to be commodified and regulated). Woody Allen movies say nothing about these kinds of social manners—the bland security of skin privilege and youth, passports through Studio 54's velvet ropes. Yet Stillman reveals the intricate rules with teensy obsession and he captures the precise tenor: "Tom's smart and somewhat cool." "You mean Departmental Dan!" "He's not without good qualities—even if very few." And when Alice and Charlotte doubt each other's friendship or casually steal a boyfriend, there's no mistaking the damage inflicted, or how such emotional alliances—like Des and Josh's antagonistic bond—persist through decorum. This isn't hedonistic—nor is it WASP-glorification. It's simply one of the most exacting movies ever made about young adult errantry.

Stillman arrived with a developed sensibility in his first film, *Metropolitan:* small gestures and fastidious, comic articulation emphasized qualities and traits that distinguish an individual within a group. His singular interest in character reveals each one's moral quest. The effort to behave decently, even by the most eccentric (self-serving) standards, gives Stillman's upperclass stories a surprising kick and a fine grain. This stems from an impulse to critique, but mainly it's personal perception of how class and individual habits clash, the result of a fresh, distinctive style. Instead of urging reform from the outside—Hollywood's typical crude assumption—Stillman has an unusual, nonjudgmental rigor. He brings movies a rare insider's sensation and dispassionate wit—as if Preston Sturges had stuck to surveying his own class origins.

Seen up close, no one in *Disco's* clique is outlandish; they're startlingly ordinary, to which Stillman lends fascination. He distills Chloë Sevigny's (Alice) calculated celebrity imprudence from the bohemian exploitation of *Kids* and *Gummo* to the truth; she's not much of an actress and garbles her early dialogue, but then settles into a perfectly cossetted young frumpiness. She's paired with the law man Josh, whom Matthew Keeslar plays as both prig and enthusiast, uncovering a tenuous social standing. Josh articulates Stillman's social impulses. "When the time came to have a social life, I wished there'd be a place to drink, dance, talk." He calls himself a "loyal adherent to the disco movement." It's hard to dislike him. His romance with Alice gives the movie a late stir, their compatibility seems a nightlife dream—but complicated by compromises adulthood forces upon them.

These are Stillman's fullest, most daring characters yet. Alice and Josh's first private talk ("I *will* take no for an answer," he tells her when she teases) contains bold, humanist risk. Describing himself as a loon, Josh recites a hymn, then makes the sound of a bird, swaying off balance as he walks down the street. "You think I'm wacko?" he asks, taking Alice inside his loneliness, and her sad look communicates a shared confidence. Contemporary movies rarely get as intimate as that, and Stillman goes further. English actress Kate Beckinsale achieves a striking American bitch transformation: sleek, haughty, and precipitate, her churning insecurities are protected by an impeccable, inherited facade. Beckinsale's Charlotte constantly abrades and one-ups her initial infatuations, yet Stillman shows a side of her character—she sings—that takes the entire comedy of manners into unexpected territory, revealing a suppressed cultural background that explains these urbane pilgrims at both their best and worst.

A rung below wealthy but still relying on family subsidy ("It's a small allowance," Charlotte notes), these white characters are charged with the capacity to be fully, infuriatingly human. That's because while admitting their advantages, Stillman has expunged the Hollywood tradition—itself a class-constructed bias—that makes us expect a caustic, dismissive, or trivializing view of the ruling class. Stillman disorients robotic viewers by presenting characters who are already caustic, dismissive, and trivializing. "The Woodstock generation was so full of itself and conceited" Charlotte sniffs. And her comment ironically pegs her own generation—if that slips by, you miss the marvel Stillman intends.

This Brooks Brothers Gibbon has claimed a specific historical moment as a result of thinking through the past two decades of New York's urbane upheaval. Many filmmakers have availed themselves of prerogative and delusion, ignoring the recession all around them, yet Stillman goes back and concentrates on forgotten details of genuine 1980s American class drudgery and evolution. This is a movie in which young folks share a railroad apartment ("These were built for working-class families, now yuppie roommate combos are crowding them out," Dan chides, and Charlotte settles it, "That's just tough."); where a young professional irons his own shirts; where nightclub small talk reveals easy snobbery and deep naiveté. *Disco* depicts the shock of worldly realization descending upon the generation that came of age after a period of intense folly— youth on the verge of smugness.

In the passionately sarcastic manner Chris Eigeman brings to Stillman's films (Des scores off the club's gratuities of cocaine and easy sex, dumping female conquests by claiming he's gay), the playboy proves to be *Disco's* most caustic prognosticator. Des wonders, "'To thine own self be true?' What if 'thine own self' is irredeemably rotten? Wouldn't it be better to not be true to thine self?" His questions challenge every opportunity that has fallen his way (or ever will), yet even this scoundrel gets one's compassion because that self-questioning is honest. Better than judging disco-era sex and drug habits, Stillman knows that social habits affect his characters' lives spiritually, profoundly. ("Come on, everybody gets something," Charlotte nags in a remorseless speech about venereal disease, and a gay couple passes in the next shot.) That's the respect Stillman pays to the period he surveys. As Josh reflects: "We can change our context, we can't change ourselves."

Josh's most heated and personal argument with Des explicates *Lady and the Tramp*, a vivid debate compressing their generation's politics and culture into an outline of the era's eventual power shifts and betrayed affections. It's hilarious but possibly the film's only miscalculation. That discussion really ought to be about disco, delving into the way one cultural parvenu says "disco sucks" to another, only waiting his chance to join in. Stillman makes genuine use of music, with no false appropriations. *The Last Days of Disco* reveals pop's cultural plurality, distinguishing Casablanca Records from Philadelphia International and appreciating both.

In Nile Rodgers and Bernard Edward's group Chic, the expression of romantic and social aspiration fabricated a vision of utopia that reached its peak in the 1979 single "Good Times." Swanky strings over funky bass notes poised ethereal ease (a fantasy) next to earthly grind (dance). That's what made disco political; musicians and dancers remade their world through rhythm and will—dialectical sensuality was an impulse felt in your pelvis and your feet. Chic's desirings (extended in hiphop by the Sugarhill Gang and De La Soul, both sampling "Good Times") are innately understood as all-American. That's why it's a splendid soundtrack for Stillman's vision of the young white educated class's gentrification. It's about that starting-out period, but uses the great presence that disco music still has to make a story of *then* relevant to *now*. Scrutinizing that phase, Stillman clarifies how we got in the mess we're in today.

From Ivy League backgrounds to new urban beginnings, Stillman's clique goes through social reengineering no different from the black urban experience Rodgers and Edwards dreamed in "Good Times," "What About Me," "Real People," "I Want Your Love," "Rebels Are We," etc,, Chic's brittle and elastic tunes, adopting Wes Montogery's insouciance to youthful drive, mark a change in black social perspective (check Chic's gorgeous "So Fine" from the neglected masterpiece "Take It Off") similar to the ambitions of Stillman's brood. The well-selected disco tunes—from Carol Douglas's "Doctor's Orders" to Cheryl Lynn's "Got To Be Real," Gwen McRae's "Rockin' Chair," and Evelyn "Champagne" King's imperishable "Shame"—provide a parallel dramatic ambiance. Chic's "Everybody Dance" is such a pleasure cushion that even bad white dancing seems graced by it. The restraint and passion in the female vocals and the dextrous arrangements on that record are, if nothing else, testimonies to black capacity and ingenuity. But the film's most discomfiting irony (for some) is that Stillman's characters realize disco tells their story, too. Stillman remembers that "regular" people killed disco (a documentary fragment preserves the fact of American homophobia and racism), but he knows that black and gay largesse, as expressed through that music, embraced all nonetheless. Call it Cosmopolitan.

WHIT STILLMAN, NOVELIST

George Sim Johnston

WE ALL KNOW THAT great novels often make bad movies. Hollywood has made a hash of *The Great Gatsby* three times and will no doubt do so again. The problem is that when screenwriters and directors try to recreate the literary pleasures of a good book, they breathe into the movie a soul made of paper and ink rather than celluloid. Mediocre novels present no such problem. It is a good thing that *Red Alert* was a forgettable paperback original, or we would not have *Dr. Strangelove*. So, a simple rule will spare you the screen versions of *Bonfire of the Vanities* and *Snow Falling on Cedars*: Love the book, skip the movie.

But what about a wonderful movie that is turned into a novel? Whit Stillman's *The Last Days of Disco* worked beautifully on the screen. Like his two previous films, *Metropolitan* and *Barcelona*, it gave the sort of pleasure one usually gets from a good foreign film. There on the screen, without subtitles, were interesting people saying witty, literate things. Stillman, in fact, achieved something novelists are supposed to do, but don't anymore: He gave us rich reportage about a fascinating social milieu—the inflamed disco culture of the early 1980s as experienced by a group of post-collegiate settlers on the island of Manhattan. And the reportage included the sufficiently complex and occasionally baffling interior lives of his subjects to make the movie satisfying on all counts.

Now he has turned *The Last Days of Disco* into a novel. I have never before read a "novelization" of a movie. I assume that the majority are inexpertly padded screenplays produced for obviously commercial purposes. However that may be, the metamorphosis of *The Last Days of*

This article originally appeared in *The American Spectator* (2000), 72-73.

Disco (the movie) into *The Last days of Disco* (the book) is as miraculous and unexpected as anything in Ovid. It is as though the author had a burden of social knowledge that he could not fully discharge in one medium and so turned into a novelist to get the job fully done. If Stillman's movies remind you of a European art film that is actually fun, this novel puts one in the mind of the good old days of elegant social fiction—of Wharton and Fitzgerald, Marquand and Cheever.

The story is told by Jimmy Steinway, who works for an ad agency in New York but whose real emotional life is among friends who gather at what is referred to only as "the Club." We are at the tail end of the Studio 54 epoch. The Club is hard to get into, and Jimmy scores points with his employer by getting clients past the velvet rope. He manages this because of his friendship with Des, a morally conflicted contemporary who helps run the place. At the Club, the real action is not on the dance floor but in the banquettes and unisex powder rooms, where a disarming set of characters engage in banter, pair off, break up, and generally go through the motions of this particular phase of the sexual revolution.

Even more than the movie, the novel is a mixed report card on how the sexual revolution has changed the relations between the sexes. The characters are all searching for intimacy and often end in bed. But the easily accessible acrobatics only seem to make the two sexes more puzzling to one another. "It's one of the aspects of the sexual revolution they don't like to talk about," says the tart, marvelously drawn Charlotte. "Men have gotten very, very weird." When Charlotte's best friend Alice has an abrupt night of passion with the environmentalist-lawyer Tom, the narrator's reflections are the perfect verbal counterpart of the bittersweet morning-after shot in the movie:

> How a young woman might feel leaving a man's house early in the morning after the first night of her first adult love affair seems to me totally mysterious and worth further study and understanding. Would she feel completely happy, joyous at having finally found someone and having that passion so quickly reciprocated, physically and emotionally fulfilled, perhaps even with the triumph of conquest and of having her femininity, skill, and allure confirmed? Or, on the other hand, would she feel vulnerable and exposed, in a strategically weak-

ened position with the man involved, and perhaps open to criticism for having moved "too quickly" and acted in a way that, from the outside in the eyes of the critical and moralistic, might have even seemed a little bit "slutty"?

Such passages (and there are many) marvelously capture the ambiguity of the new sexual freedoms. Jimmy and his male friends want the quick revelations of an affair, but also seem to agree with Henry James that the most appealing women are those possessing both "mystery and manners." (Yes, there is a double standard here.) As a result, they gravitate toward the incorrigibly demur Alice. Alice herself has a properly old-fashioned aunt on whom she tries to model herself, and there is a devastating scene toward the end when the aunt tearfully reveals to Alice over lunch how she has caught her supposedly wonderful husband in the act of adultery. In that moment, an entire world of WASP propriety and respect comes to grief.

If romance in the Age of Disco does not quite satisfy, there are the added frustrations of earning a living in a city which has not yet discovered leveraged buyouts, let alone entered cyberspace. Stillman gives us a marvelous portrait of a group of intelligent and sensitive people improvising their third decade in the job market. Three of them work for a publishing house that doesn't pay much but at least keeps lit their literary pilot lights. Another, Josh, works for the Manhattan district attorney and ends up busting the Club's owner for drugs and tax evasion. He has spent his professional life waiting for a climactic moment when he could say, "Book this clown!" and so achieves the most vocational satisfaction. And there is Des, who is a wonderful creation. Everyone who went to college in the early 1970s knows him. He would like to spend his life watching television and doing drugs and lands a job in the downtown club scene which is highly compatible with both pursuits.

This being a Stillmanesque production, it is no surprise to discover at the end that this highly talkative bunch have been secretly maturing into solid bourgeoisie all along. The narrator is rightly annoyed that the 1980s are always referred to as the Decade of Greed. So far as he is concerned, the early 1980s were a time of hard work and maximum productivity. They were, in fact, "the young-adult Wonder Years...." The narrator adds that "it's not as if we have so many decades that we can afford to go around trashing them for no very good reason."

Tom Wolfe once complained that the hippie subculture did not produce a single good novel. Not even a rivulet of tepid prose issued from the typewriters of acid freaks. Until now, the same could be said of disco. Dickens and Thackeray would have had no complaints about the abundant novelistic material available on the dance floors of Studio 54, Heartbreak, and all those raffish music holes south of Fourteenth Street. With adroit dialogue, marvelous scene-painting, and sharp character-sketching, Stillman has delivered an era that was not so long ago but seems to have sunk beneath the pavement like a lost Atlantis.

Index

A

"A Mighty Fortress Is Our God" 59
Academy Award xi, 20
Adams, George Matthew 111
Agee, Philip 27
Alain-Fournier, Henry 41
Alice 11-14, 17, 32-36, 42, 120, 122-
    127, 129, 131, 140-147, 162-
    164, 168, 169
Alighieri, Dante 126
Allen, Gracie 29
Allen, Woody 163
"Amazing Grace" 14, 17, 120, 125,
    129, 131, 144, 145, 147
American Beauty 100
Astin, Mackenzie 11. See also
    Steinway, Jimmy
Atlantis 170
Audrey. See Rouget, Audrey
Aurora 10, 92, 95, 96, 107, 108,
    110, 111
Austen, Jane 1-3, 5, 12, 13, 15,
    16, 40, 44, 45, 51, 133, 138,
    139, 151

B

Babar 24
Babette's Feast 100

Baby Boomers 35
Badia, Nuria 10. See also Aurora
Band of Outsiders 151
Barcelona xii, xiii, xvi, 2, 3, 7, 9,
    26, 27, 43, 89, 94, 95, 101,
    102, 110, 112, 114, 120, 154,
    156, 159, 160
Barrie, J. M. 42
Barry, Philip 157
Bayaka Pygmies 149
Beckinsale, Kate 11, 164. See also
    Pingree, Charlotte
BeeGees 109
Bergen, Tushka 8. See also Mont-
    serrat
Bernie 36, 127, 128
Bettger, Frank 94, 95, 101, 110,
    111, 157
Beverly Hills Ninja 100
Bible 8, 13, 29, 44, 93, 101, 105,
    110, 155, 156
Black, Charlie 3, 5, 6, 7, 13, 14,
    16, 21, 24, 25, 39, 40, 45,
    56, 57, 59-66, 71-75, 77, 78,
    80-83, 150-153
Bloom, Allan 135, 137
Bonfire of the Vanities 167
Boynton, Fred 2, 3, 7-11, 15, 16,

22, 26, 28-30, 33, 43-45,
88-97, 100-106, 110-112, 114,
154-160
Boynton, Ted xv, 2, 3, 7, 8-11,
15, 16, 26, 27, 28, 29, 29-
30, 33, 43, 44, 45, 88-97, 100-
105, 107-114, 154-160
Brook Farm 45, 65, 66, 83
Brutus 128
Bulwer-Lytton, Sir Edward 119
Buñuel, Luis 16, 21

C

Caesar 128
Cahiers du Cinéma 152
Cambridge 46
Cannes Film Festival 20
Carnegie, Dale 8, 20, 29, 94, 95,
101, 108, 110, 157
Casablanca Records 165
Cash, Johnny 157
Cerberus 126, 128
Charlie. See Black, Charlie
Charlotte. See Pingree, Charlotte
Cheever, John 168
Chesterton, G. K. 119
Chic 165
Chicago 3, 10, 92, 94, 101, 154, 158
Chloë Sevigny. See Alice
Clarke, Jane
5, 22, 23, 56, 57, 59, 60, 61,
66, 68-70, 72, 76-79, 150
Clements, Edward 2. See also
Townsend, Tom
Clueless 51
Coen (Coen Brothers) 156
Cold War xiv, 7, 29, 88, 100, 154
Cruise, Tom 29
Cukor, George 154, 157
Cukor on Cukor 154
Curtis, Richard 156
Cynthia. See McLean, Cynthia

D

Dalai Lama 12
De La Soul 166
"Dear Lord and Father of Mankind"
42, 142
Death of a Salesman 29, 94, 157
Decline of the West 3
Democracy In America 81
Democratic Party 20
"Departmental" Dan
138, 139, 163, 165
Des. See McGrath, Des
Dickens, Charles 170
*Discreet Charm of the Bourgeoisie,
The* 16, 21
Disney xiii, 35, 134
"Doctor's Orders" 166
Douglas, Carol 166
Dr. Strangelove 167
Drucker, Peter 109

E

Economist, The 8, 15, 155
Edward, Bernard 165
Edwards, Dick 60, 66, 67
Effective Executive, The 95
Eigeman, Chris 2, 4, 11, 152, 159,
165. See also Boynton,
Fred; McGrath, Des; Smith,
Nick
Eliot, T. S. xv, 87, 119
Emerson, Ralph Waldo 29, 94, 101
Emma 51
Essay on Man 36
"Everybody Dance" 166

F

Farina, Carolyn 2, 152. See also
Rouget, Audrey
Fitzgerald, F. Scott 150, 168

Four Weddings and a Funeral
    156, 159
Fourier, Charles
    2, 6, 21, 45, 83, 150
Fowler, Sally 5, 68, 76, 150
Franco, Francisco 43, 45
Franklin, Benjamin 8, 9, 29, 94, 101
Fred. See Boynton, Fred
Fukuyama, Francis 137
Fuller, Margaret 87

G

Gaudí, Antonio 156
Gillies, Isabel 5. See also McLean,
    Cynthia
God 8-10, 13, 14, 77, 105, 106,
    135, 142, 144
Godard, Jean Luc 151, 160
Goethe, Johann Wolfgang von 87,
    89
"Good Times" 162, 166
"Got To Be Real" 166
Graduate, The 96, 156
Grand Central Station 23, 74
Grant, Hugh 156
Great Gatsby, The 167
Greenleaf, John Whittier 42
Greta 10, 92, 109, 158
Gross, Terry 20, 31
Gummo 163

H

Hampshire College xiii, 133
Hampton, Lionel 87, 108, 156
Hampton, Vinyl 92, 105, 108, 110,
    156
Harvard xii, xiii, 31, 34, 42, 133,
    142, 146, 162
Heartbreak 170
Hegel, G. W. F. 136
Hemingway, Ernest 127
Hoffman, Dustin 96

*How I Raised Myself from Failure to
    Success in Sales* 8
Howard, Sidney 87
Hudsucker Proxy, The 156
Hundley, Dylan 5. See also Fowler,
    Sally
Huston, Walter 87

I

"I Want Your Love" 166
IHSMOCO. See Illinois High-Speed
    Motor Corporation
Illinois High-Speed Motor Corpora-
    tion 7, 29, 90, 92, 94, 108, 109

J

Jack. See Tyrrell, Jack
James, Henry 87, 169
Jane. See Clarke, Jane
Jarmusch, Jim 157
Jimmy. See Steinway, Jimmy
"Jingle Bells" 78
Johnson, Samuel 1, 43, 44, 110
Josh. See Neff, Josh

K

Keeslar, Matt 11, 163. See also Neff,
    Josh
Kempe, Will 4. See also Sloneker,
    Rick von
Kids 163
King, Evelyn "Champagne" 166

L

Lady and the Tramp
    12, 35, 134, 142, 165
Lasch, Christopher 136
*Last Days of Disco, With Cocktails at
    Petrossian Afterwards, The* 19
Lawrence, D. H. 87

Leonard, Robert Sean 11. See also
     Platt, Tom
Lewis, Sinclair 87
Lincoln, Abraham 83
"Little Gidding" 119
Livingstone, Cathy 57
Locke, John 136
Looking for Mr. Goodbar 33
Love in the Ruins xvi
"Love Train" 131, 147
Luther, Martin 59
Lynn, Cheryl 166

M

Mackenzie, Astin. See Steinway,
     Jimmy
Manhattan xii, 2, 3, 11, 14, 20,
     31, 36, 39, 50, 54, 71, 133,
     167, 169
Mansfield Park 4, 8, 51-55, 151
Marcuse, Herbert 135
Marquand, J. P. 168
Marta 9, 11, 90-93, 102, 105, 106,
     110, 112, 113, 159
Marx, Karl 63
McGrath, Des 11, 13-16, 34, 35,
     36, 42, 120, 121, 125-130,
     134, 141, 147, 148, 162, 163,
     165, 168, 169
McLean, Cynthia 5, 15, 24, 54, 56,
     57, 59, 72, 77-79, 150, 152
McRae, Gwen 166
Miller, Arthur 29, 30, 94
Miller, Glenn 8, 29, 42, 44, 93, 155
Mira Sorvino. See Marta
Mitford, Nancy 123
Montserrat 8, 10, 27, 28, 30, 33,
     89-92, 95, 105-109, 110, 113,
     155, 158, 159
More, Thomas xvi
Munne, Pep 8. See also Ramon
Music Man, The 21
Mussolini, Benito 91

N

National Public Radio 20
Naylor, Thomas H. 49
Neff, Fred 150, 152
Neff, Josh 11-17, 31-37, 42, 43,
     120, 125-129, 131, 142-
     146, 147, 162-165
New York Magazine 6, 57
Newell, Mike 156
Newton-John, Olivia 137
Nichols, Mike 96
Nichols, Taylor 2, 3, 152, 159. See
     also Boynton, Ted
Nick. See Smith, Nick
Nouveau Monde Industriel, Le 45

O

"O Come All Ye Faithful" 78
O'Connor, Flannery 129
Old Testament 8, 155
Only Angels Have Wings 157
Orwell, George 90
Ovid 168

P

Parisi, Allison 5. See also Clarke,
     Jane
Peanuts 50
Perceval 157
Percy, Walker xvi
Perkins, Polly 4-5, 6, 57
Persuasion 70, 80
Philadelphia International Records
     165
Pine Manor College 46
Pingree, Charlotte 11, 12, 14, 17,
     32-36, 122-131, 141,
     143-147, 162-165, 168
Platt, Tom
     33, 123, 124, 126, 163, 168
Polonius 128

Pompeii 119
Pope, Alexander 36
Price, Fanny 52, 54
Pride and Prejudice 1, 2
Psychology Today 46, 133
Pulp Fiction 104

R

Ramon 8, 10, 11, 15, 16, 27-
    30, 90-92, 97, 104-114
Reagan, Ronald 102, 139
"Real People" 166
"Rebels Are We" 166
Risky Business 29
"Rockin' Chair" 166
Rodgers, Nile 165
Rohmer, Eric 151, 160
Ross, Katherine 96
Rouget, Audrey 2, 4-8, 15, 21,
    40, 49, 50-54, 59-62, 64,
    150, 151
Rousseau, Jean-Jacques 100

S

Sade, Marquis de 8, 43, 110
Saint Francis 24
Saint-Gardens, Augustus 87
Salinger, J. D. 11, 41, 134
Sally Fowler Rat Pack xii, 4-6,
    21-24, 51, 54, 56, 63, 65,
    72, 74, 75, 77, 80, 149
San Francisco 102
Saturday Night Fever 136
Scarlet Pimpernel, The 158
Schmied, Hellena 10, 159. See also
    Greta
Scrooge McDuck
    33, 120, 123, 124, 134
Sense and Sensibility 133
Serena. See Slocum, Serena
Sevigny, Chloë 11, 163. See also
    Alice

SFRP. See Sally Fowler Rat Pack
Shakespeare, William xvi, 114
"Shame" 166
Simpsons, The 20
Sinatra, Frank 5
Slocum, Serena 6-7, 51, 53, 54,
    60, 66, 68, 69, 71, 76, 77,
    80, 150
Sloneker, Rick von 4-8, 23, 24, 53,
    56-60, 62, 72, 74, 78, 80, 150
Smith, Nick 4, 4-6, 15, 22, 24,
    40, 41, 50, 54-56, 58, 59,
    62, 64, 65, 67, 71,-75, 77,
    81, 101, 150, 152
Snow Falling on Cedars 167
"So Fine" 166
Sorvino, Mira 9. See also Marta
Southampton 6, 25, 60, 71, 78, 83
Spengler, Oswald 3, 94
St. Regis Hotel 22, 74
St. Thomas Episcopal Church 78
Steinway, Jimmy 11, 20, 34-36,
    120, 122, 125-129, 162, 168,
    169
Stillman, Whit xi, xiii, xiv, xvi, 1,
    3, 20, 31, 45, 46, 131, 133, 157,
    159, 164
Studio 54 136, 162, 163, 168, 170
Sturges, Preston 163
Sugarhill Gang 166
Summers, Donna 108, 155
Sundance Film Festival 49

T

"Take It Off" 166
Tarantino, Quentin 104, 155
Tate, Allen xv
Taylor, Dickie 10, 90, 94, 96, 111
Ted. See Boynton, Ted
Thackeray, William Makepeace 32,
    170
The Effective Executive 8
Thomas, John 151, 156

Thompson, Elizabeth 6. See also
    Slocum, Serena
Thomson, James Alexander Kerr 19
Tocqueville, Alexis de 10, 81, 140
Tolstoy, Leo 1, 158
Tom. See Townsend, Tom
Townsend, Tom 2, 4, 6, 7, 11, 15,
    16, 21–23, 40, 41, 45, 50-
    62, 65, 66, 68, 69, 70-79,
    83, 150-152
Travolta, John 136, 137
Trilling, Lionel 40, 51, 151
Tyrrell, Jack 108

U

U.H.B. See urban haute bourgeoisie
Uncle Scrooge. See Scrooge McDuck
urban haute bourgeoisie xiii, 3, 4,
    7, 24-26, 34, 36, 39, 40, 46,
    59, 62, 64, 81, 82, 133-139,
    148, 151

V

Van 126, 128
Veblen, Thorstein 2, 21, 40
Vespucci, Amerigo 87

W

War and Peace 64, 74, 79, 158
Washington, George 9
WASP 24, 39, 59, 63, 163, 169
"Wasteland, The" xv
Wharton, Edith 168
"What About Me" 166
Wilder, Billy 156
Willimon, William H. 49
Wolfe, Tom 170